CHASE

CATALOGS
1934 AND 1935

Introduction by Leslie Piña
and Donald-Brian Johnson

Price guide by Barry L. Van Hook

Schiffer Publishing Ltd

880 Lower Valley Road, Atglen, PA 19310 USA

CHROMIUM
BRASS & COPPER
SPECIALTIES

Acknowledgments

Our sincere appreciation to Olga Laylon and the late Harry Laylon, Chase Director of Design, for making these catalogs available. Without their preservation efforts, an important component of the Deco heritage would have been lost.

Our gratitude to Barry L. Van Hook of the Chase Collectors Society, for invaluable assistance in preparation of the price guide.

Special thanks also, for advice, encouragement, and expertise, to: Enrique Conill; Barbara and Dale Endter; Raechel Guest, Assistant Curator, Mattatuck Museum; Mr. and Mrs. Charles M. Johnson, Sr; Chuck Kaplan; Chris Kennedy; Steve Klender; Hank Kuhlmann; Paula Ockner; Bill Pierce; Ramón Piña; Gary M. Piper; Jill Thomas-Clark; John and Donna Thorpe; Chuck and Kim Zuccarini; Peter Schiffer, Douglas Congdon-Martin, Bruce Waters, Bonnie M. Hensley, and the staff at Schiffer Publishing.

Published by Schiffer Publishing Ltd.
4880 Lower Valley Road
Atglen, PA 19310
Phone: (610) 593-1777; Fax: (610) 593-2002
E-mail: Schifferbk@aol.com
Please write for a free catalog.
This book may be purchased from the publisher.
Please include $3.95 for shipping.

In Europe, Schiffer books are distributed by
Bushwood Books
6 Marksbury Avenue
Kew Gardens
Surrey TW9 4JF England
Phone: 44 (0) 181 392-8585; Fax: 44 (0) 181 392-9876
E-mail: Bushwd@aol.com

Please try your bookstore first.

We are interested in hearing from authors
with book ideas on related subjects.

Designed by Leslie Piña & Donald-Brian Johnson
Layout by Bonnie M. Hensley

ISBN: 0-7643-0631-6
Printed in China

Introduction

American Art Deco

There are two distinct phases of American modernism. Both are rich in cultural history, and both have yielded an abundance of decorative arts that continues to fascinate collectors and admirers. The first phase, called Art Deco, came to the United States from Europe in the late 1920s and then adapted to the culture of the Depression era in the 1930s. The next period, which is known as the "postwar" era or "mid-century," gave us some of the century's most remarkable furniture design, followed by wildly innovative pottery and an assortment of other interior furnishings. The most collectible of these postwar items were mass produced and ranged from tongue-in-cheek kitsch to high style industrial design, soon displayed in museums.

Although this second phase of modernism was the more widespread and popular, it was dependent on the Art Deco period style. Actually, Art Deco includes a complex range of styles that evolved from the earlier French *Art Nouveau*. Tired of the historic revivals and arbitrary eclecticism of the Victorian period, designers consciously sought a "new art," hence, *Art Nouveau*. Characterized by asymmetrical organic forms, with a Japanese design influence at its best, and a relapse into the excesses of French Rococo at its — well, other extreme, this new art soon bored its clientele. By the time of World War I, it was succeeded by another French elitist handicraft style. Not only newness, but modernity was its theme, and Art Moderne (modern art) replaced asymmetry with symmetry, nature with geometry, and Rococo with Neoclassical references. In Europe, especially France, Art Moderne remained a handicraft employing exotic materials such as ivory, shagreen (shark skin), and rare tropical woods. The style achieved international recognition at *L'Exposition des Arts Decoratifs et Industriels Modernes* in Paris in 1925 and then soon lost its European audience.

The United States was only an observer, not a participant, at the Paris Exposition, the milestone event that has been credited with the introduction of modern decorative and industrial arts to the world. When Secretary of Commerce Herbert Hoover received the French invitation to show American modern art, he declined, but appointed a group of delegates from manufacturing, retail, and decorating fields to visit the show and report back on what America was missing. Their return home from Paris late in 1925 marked the beginning of an Americanized *Art Moderne*, or as it was later named with reference to the exposition, Art Deco.

French *Art Moderne* was not popular in America because of its high cost and because American designers were struggling to develop a native style. Almost immediately after the Paris Exposition, Art Deco entered New York via the display windows of major department stores. Fashion — clothing, accessories, perfume bottles, and furnishings used as props — caught the eye and the imagination of the American consumer. But rather than imitate the European version, dependent upon costly materials and crafting techniques, American designers borrowed only the appearance. The new look could be achieved at no more cost than the overworked historic and bland generic "styles" it soon replaced. Art Deco graphic design quickly appeared in periodicals and posters. But a truly Americanized commercialized version of the style developed when a group of graphic designers began to apply their skills to the emerging field of design for industry. Infatuated by mass-production, speed, metallic sparkle, and the new age that they represented, these American designers took the French look and transformed it. From architecture to plastic jewelry to chromium plated household items, American Art Deco applied to industrial design had the distinction of becoming the first original modern American art form.

Not only did American producers replace handicraft with industrial methods, they adapted the style's visual elements. Soft curves, stylized flowers, leaping gazelles and seductive nudes were more difficult to manufacture than the new design repertoire of geometric forms. American industrial designers developed their own design cliches of rounded corners with three parallel lines signifying streamlining, a stepped or tiered pattern resembling a skyline of skyscrapers, and a more athletic, less seductive, female dancing nude. The geometry of Cubism replaced traditional representational motifs. With additional design elements from ancient Egypt, Pre-Columbian Mexico, some less-explainable European peasant art, and the austerity of the German Bauhaus, American Art Deco was presented to the consumer. With factory production techniques and subsequent affordability, the new modern look could brighten an otherwise drab American home.

Chase Tower, 10 East 40th Street, New York City. (The artist's conception of this photo is on opposite page.)

What the designers created were not just industrially made household products, but a new form of art. This machine-made art had obvious advantages over handicraft: it could be made more economically, more quickly, and more consistently. It was accessible to the American consumer whose finances, but not desires, had been destroyed by the Depression. Smooth, shiny surfaces with little or no ornamentation were designed by a new type of designer who entered the new profession equipped with both vision and marketing skills. If Depression-weary consumers could no longer afford traditional art, then the definition was changed to include machine art as well. Anyone could afford to own some machine art, and it seemed as if everyone did.

As a result of this modern merger between art and industry (and philosophy) a new field of industrial design developed, especially in America in the 1930s. The initial goal of industrial design was to transform ordinary household items into extraordinary objects of desire by making them both visually appealing and affordable. It represented the antithesis of elitist handicraft, because industrial design required mass production techniques. Its streamlined style, however, was based not only on aerodynamics but on French Art Deco. The irony is twofold: many of the products were unrelated to transportation — why make a toaster with the same aerodynamic styling as a train? — and Art Deco design originally focused on luxury art and not utility. Logical or not, the results were often dazzling.

Lurelle Guild and Walter Von Nessen were two of the American pioneer professional industrial designers to translate aspects of French Art Deco to an American vernacular and methods of industrial production. Guild was one of the most prolific of the early designers, and among his many accomplishments was a collection of smooth, satiny aluminum decorative and utilitarian items made by Alcoa in New Kensington, Pennsylvania, called Kensington Ware. The initial line was introduced in 1934, one year after the Chase Brass & Copper Co. offered its first major product catalog of machine art specialty items. Guild designed for Alcoa's Kensington and for Chase simultaneously throughout the 1930s, and many of the designs bear a close resemblance to each other.

Interior Display, Chase Tower. (Opposite is the artist's rendition of this scene.)

Walter Von Nessen, another well-known pioneer industrial designer, also freelanced for Chase, and many other talented designers — from free-lancers Russel Wright and Rockwell Kent, to Chase staff designer Harry Laylon — helped create more than just the product of one remarkable company. These designers achieved a look that characterized the decade — and it became one of the most significant decades in the history of American decorative art and design. Not all Depression era, or even all Chase, design was Art Deco. But many of the forms designed for Chase have come to epitomize the best American Art Deco machine art. Their chromium finish helped make both the product and the period shine.

Leslie Piña, Ph.D.
March 1998

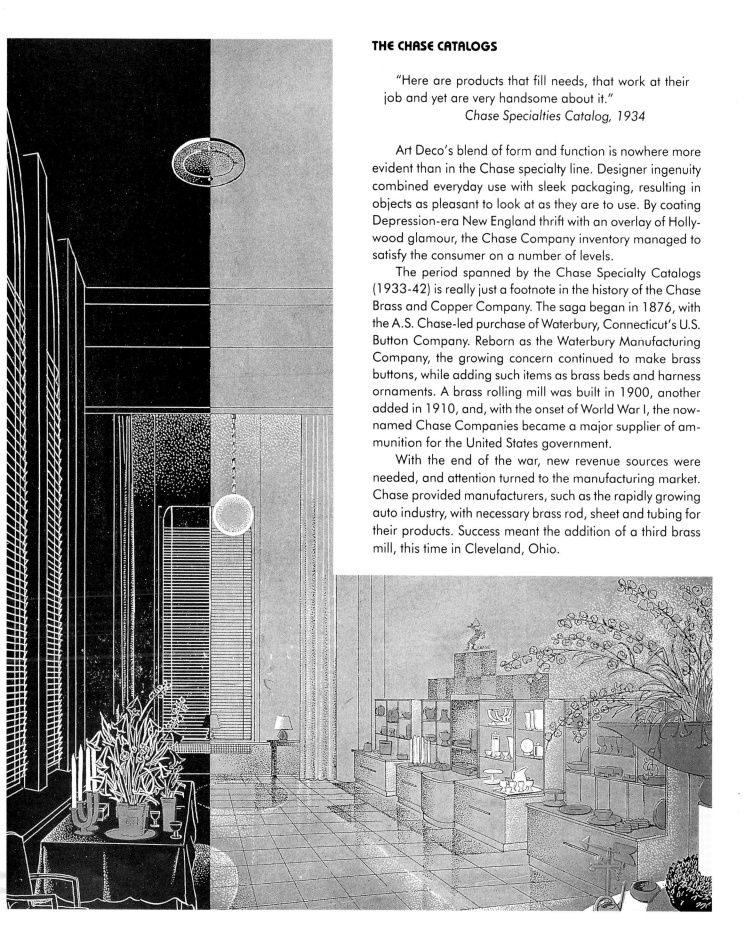

THE CHASE CATALOGS

"Here are products that fill needs, that work at their job and yet are very handsome about it."
Chase Specialties Catalog, 1934

Art Deco's blend of form and function is nowhere more evident than in the Chase specialty line. Designer ingenuity combined everyday use with sleek packaging, resulting in objects as pleasant to look at as they are to use. By coating Depression-era New England thrift with an overlay of Hollywood glamour, the Chase Company inventory managed to satisfy the consumer on a number of levels.

The period spanned by the Chase Specialty Catalogs (1933-42) is really just a footnote in the history of the Chase Brass and Copper Company. The saga began in 1876, with the A.S. Chase-led purchase of Waterbury, Connecticut's U.S. Button Company. Reborn as the Waterbury Manufacturing Company, the growing concern continued to make brass buttons, while adding such items as brass beds and harness ornaments. A brass rolling mill was built in 1900, another added in 1910, and, with the onset of World War I, the now-named Chase Companies became a major supplier of ammunition for the United States government.

With the end of the war, new revenue sources were needed, and attention turned to the manufacturing market. Chase provided manufacturers, such as the rapidly growing auto industry, with necessary brass rod, sheet and tubing for their products. Success meant the addition of a third brass mill, this time in Cleveland, Ohio.

The Chase Specialty Shop, Chase Tower. (The artist's illustration is found opposite.)

The move from providing manufacturers with component parts to providing the private consumer with finished product was a direct result of the Depression. With sales to manufacturers slackening, other avenues needed to be explored. Mass-producing inexpensive, yet attractive and practical, household items proved a workable option.

As 1930s America moved full speed ahead into a streamlined future, anything contributing toward that move found widespread acceptance. Thanks to Chase's introduction of chromium specialties, a hostess could escape the drudgery of polishing silver, yet still manage to set a sparkling table — and she could do so economically. While stressing that chromium did not "compete with solid silver," Chase promotional releases of the time were also quick to point out the metal's main advantage over its more costly cousin:

Here is a metal that will not tarnish or blacken. Wash chromium with a soapy cloth, just as you would china.

Rub lightly with a dry cloth and every finger mark disappears. No more cleaning with dirty greasy rags. No more acid polishes and pastes that get under fingernails and make hands rough and dry. Chromium keeps shining and brilliant and is always ready to use. Chromium stays polished.

And it didn't rust either. Unlike its competitors, Chase plated a chrome finish over a nickel-plated brass or copper base. No rust? No tarnish? No housewife could resist! Ease of care was a major selling point, and remained a basic tenet of Chase advertising over the years.

Beginning with its first complete catalog (1933's "Giftwares"), Chase embarked on full-scale production of its specialty line — production that would continue with great success until the outbreak of World War II. From coffee sets to candlesticks, serving trays to smoking accessories, items included in the Chase catalogs indicate the important role home entertaining played in 1930s social life. If Depression finances precluded lavish dinners out, why not simulate the experience at a fraction of the cost? Chase's in-house and freelance designers were kept busy churning out a dizzying array of objects needed to suggest the ambiance of a fine dining establishment. The 1934 catalog alone lists nearly one dozen different trays, each with its own carefully defined function. What party-giver would think of serving cheese on anything other than the Chase "Cheese Server Tray" (#09010)? As the copy points out:

> There are certain good old rules for serving cheese. Cheese should be placed and cut on wood. It should be covered. And it should appear together with its crackers. This cheese server does all these things, and looks handsome besides.

After a description like that, would you settle for anything less?

More variety of course meant more sales. To increase the profit margin, designers were also encouraged to use component parts from the Chase inventory in new and innovative ways. Those enjoying the simple lines of the "Glow Lamp" (#01001) or the "Rain-Beau Watering Can" (#05002), for instance, may be surprised to learn of their humble origins as Chase copper toilet floats!

While ten years' worth of specialty catalogs are known to exist, those selected for reproduction here — 1934 and 1935 — have been chosen for the very specific contrasts they represent. In 1934, Chase was still gauging just what its customers would find most appealing. There's a "homey" feel to the 1934 catalog, with its no-nonsense photography of an inventory mixing the mundane ("The Duplex Pinpack — a modern safety pin package that belongs in a woman's handbag") with more decorative offerings. Etiquette maven Emily Post is even on hand to dish out helpful advice to "Mrs. 3-in-1", the homemaker who must be "cook and

A stylized depiction of the first Chase Specialty Shop, Chase Tower, New York City.

waitress as well as hostess." Mrs. Post's booklet, "How to Give Buffet Suppers" came with each "Electric Buffet Server" purchased, and even the domestically inept could comprehend its no-nonsense instructions:

Perhaps, as at a dance, the men fill the plates and bring them to their partners. This is what they are supposed to do. If they don't, then you have to direct them as you would direct children at a party by saying, "*Please* go into the dining room and help yourself to what you like." Then if they stand blockading the table, you have to say, "Won't you *please* take your plate and go to the other room again and sit down?"

By 1935, Mrs. 3-in-1 evidently wanted a bit of glamour to dress up her practicality. The Duplex Pinpack is gone from the 1935 catalog, replaced with such new entries as a Rockwell Kent-designed Wine Cooler and Cigarette Box. The copy for 1934's "Diplomat Coffee Set" now carries the added note that it has "appeared in well-known Broadway plays, and in some of the most popular moving pictures" and that "well-known theatrical stars and society leaders have chosen it for their drawing rooms". Retailers are urged to visit the impressive new show rooms at Chase Tower, 10 East 40th Street, New York City. And a more restrained Mrs. Post, while reiterating her 1934 observation that "chromium is the answer to the housewife's prayer—it stays brilliantly polished to the end of time," eliminates less appetizing earlier references to hazards presented by "greasy smoke from a frying pan."

The 1935 catalog design is also more opulent, with brass tint on the endpapers and drawings of the Chase building, and object photos artistically enhanced for dramatic appeal. Note the "Chase Electric Buffet Server" (#27011), on page 6 of the 1934 catalog, page 4 of the 1935. While 1934's illustration is a clear and perfectly acceptable reference photo, 1935's is a glamour shot. Floating on a dark background, chrome highlights leap out at the viewer. This glorified serving dish is as lovingly presented as any Hollywood starlet.

Which approach was more successful? That will depend on the reader's personal taste. From a historical standpoint though, it's worth noting that by 1937 the glamour shots had disappeared. Practicality reasserted itself for the remainder of the Chase Specialty years.

World War II necessitated a return to the manufacture of defense materials, and after the war Chase found a public no longer enthralled by Deco design. The company reverted solely to its profitable production of brass rod. Today, from corporate headquarters in Montpelier, Ohio, the Chase centaur presides over an industrial present, and memories of an artistic past.

Donald-Brian Johnson
March, 1998

CHASE CHROMIUM
BRASS & COPPER
PRODUCTS FOR THE
1934
SEASON

CHASE

CHASE BRASS & COPPER CO. INC. WATERBURY CONNECTICUT

Chase Brass & Copper Co., Incorporated

Specialty Sales Division

200 Fifth Avenue   New York, N. Y.

1934

Chase Chromium, Brass and Copper Products

In presenting its new line of giftwares, table-wares, and novelties for the 1934 season, Chase calls particular attention to the rising popularity of buffet meals.

Mrs. Emily Post, author of "Etiquette," "Personality of a House," etc., and known to every reader of magazines, newspapers, and to every radio listener, says—

"The present enthusiasm for every variety of buffet party would seem to be at least one happy result of the depression, which in shortening the purses of all of us, has brought appreciation of the simpler hospitalities. But whatever the cause, it is certainly true that among the nicest parties possible to give, the buffet luncheon, dinner or supper is far and away the most popular and smart. Moreover, its popularity is equally typical of the great houses and of the last word in pent-house apartments, as it is of the simplest cottage, whose owner has to be cook and waitress as well as hostess; in short, three persons in one. For Mrs. 3-in-1 the buffet table is ideal, since it makes the inviting of twenty or thirty

easily practicable when a sit-down dinner or lunch party at the dining table would be limited to eight, or perhaps as few as six! Moreover, lack of service is not a handicap and the menu can be of the simplest and the least expensive, since the great appeal of a buffet party is its friendly informality.

"On the other hand, a buffet table differently set is equally suitable on occasions that are to the highest degree formal.

"As I have already said, the depression was no doubt responsible for the buffet-supper craze, but now that its popularity is in full swing, it would seem safe to predict that even though the new deal brings prosperity back, buffet parties are too thoroughly in accord with the spirit of the present day to go out of fashion. They are far more likely to be further glorified, than to give way to returning formality."

There is no question but that the buffet meal will be popular this year. It is inexpensive to give. Any number of guests can be asked. They can

come late or early, and the food will be hot and easy to serve.

For the buffet lunch, or supper, Chase has designed an entirely new line of chromium articles. They are modern in feeling and yet harmonious with the knives, forks, plates, furniture and setting of the average home. Chromium that doesn't need polishing. Chromium that is moderate in price. Chromium that is new, smart and popular. That is the basis of the Chase line for 1934.

In the following pages notice how cleverly the modern feeling has been incorporated in the new Chase articles without that "arty" look that whispers "gadget" to a critical customer. Here are products that fill needs, that work at their job and yet are handsome about it. Here are trays that are large but not bulky; platters that hold enough cold meats, and pitchers that pour properly. If cheese is to be served there is useful wood to cut it on. You will find lamps that really give enough light; cocktail shakers that strain back fruit pulp, and hold an adequate amount without refilling.

These new Chase products are useful, but their utility has not been allowed to interfere with their design. The best of American designers—artists like Walter Von Nessen, Lurelle Guild, the Gerths, and others, have carefully styled these products in the 1934 spirit. Notice the absence of tricky decoration, meaningless knobs, embossing or etched prettiness. Here is the purity of line and definiteness of curve that shows the sure hand of the master designer. When lines of decoration are needed to carry out the spirit of the article, they are used simply and successfully.

This year Chase starts national advertising. Vogue, House & Garden, Good Housekeeping, the New Yorker, and other well-known magazines will carry photographs of Chase articles in natural colors into every home, and your customers will know and ask for these by name.

Consider your stock carefully, for Chase chromium articles for buffet meals, and Chase smoking novelties, lamps and giftwares, will be more popular than ever this year.

HOW TO ORDER

The prices listed under each item are retail prices. The wholesale prices are listed on last three pages, and are subject to change without notice.

All articles wholesaling at $7.20 a dozen, or less, are sold in dozen lots.

The minimum order accepted by us is $10.00 for accounts now on our books, and $25.00 from new accounts.

TERMS: 2% discount will be allowed on all invoices paid on or before the tenth of month following date of shipment, F. O. B. factory, Waterbury, Conn.

SALES TAX: If a sales tax is enacted, it will be added to the invoice covering the shipment of any article referred to in this catalog.

Chase Brass & Copper Co., Inc.
Specialty Sales Division

200 Fifth Avenue   New York, N. Y.

General Offices of the Chase organization at Waterbury, Connecticut.

Chase Factory where chromium, brass and copper products are made.

The largest of the Chase mills where brass and copper are cast. Located in Waterbury, Conn.

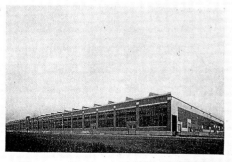

The huge Chase mill at Cleveland, Ohio, is completely equipped with modern machinery.

CHASE ELECTRIC BUFFET SERVER

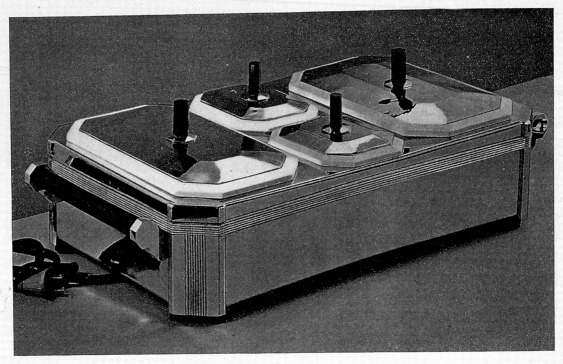

CHASE ELECTRIC BUFFET SERVER. No. 27011

Chase Brass and Copper Company announce the most useful and important addition to table service in many years. Here is an electrically heated hot dish that makes it possible, for the first time, to keep *four different kinds of food* hot on the buffet table without *overcooking.*

Mrs. Emily Post says of the new Chase Buffet Server:

"There is now a very last word in buffet equipment— the debutante daughter, as it were, of the chef's bain-marie, or a four compartment chafing dish. Its designer has called it a 'buffet server.' But no matter what it is called, it is quite the most delectable novelty that has been produced; to me at least, it is completely tempting. Its design is modernistic, as is suitable in the polished chromium of which it is made, and yet its simplicity of design that relies for its ornamentation on octagon out-

line and ivory edging and ebony handles, would be entirely in key with almost any type of house. It holds four deep casserole dishes, two large and two small, set into a smart tray shaped box filled with water kept by an electric element at an exact temperature. No metal, it seems to me, is quite so complete an answer to the housewife's prayer as chromium—appealing not only to the eye, but to practical requirements, because unless subjected to gas or to greasy smoke from a frying pan, it stays brilliantly polished to the end of time. Another beauty of chromium to most of us, is that really lovely things can be had at comparatively small expense."

Description

The Chase electric buffet server is a giant hot water dish, half filled with water which is kept between 160° and 180° by a concealed electric heating element. Into the receptacle with its electrically heated water are placed four porcelain casserole dishes, two large (2½ quart capacity) and two small (1½ pint capacity). These dishes each have their chromium cover with black composition handle. The server itself has two long composition bar handles so that the server can be moved easily from place to place. It operates on either A. C. or D. C. current, 110 to 120 volt circuit, 25, 40 or 60 cycles, and has a current consumption of 1/7 kilowatt per hour. Over-all, the server is 18 inches long, 11 inches wide and 5 inches high.

Design

The Chase Buffet Server was created by Lurelle Guild. In brilliant chromium and lustrous black, its modern lines and shape make it one of the most important articles ever designed for the supper table. It was made to answer the request of hundreds of worried hostesses who "wished there was something made to keep things hot and attractive for late guests." Here it is!

Mechanical Operation

To fill the server the casseroles are removed and the server is filled with boiling water up to the water line clearly marked along the side of the interior. The electric plug is then attached to the regular house electric circuit in the outlet used for the electric toaster or coffee percolator, or in any convenient base receptacle outlet.

The casserole dishes are filled with their proper foods in the kitchen, and brought in and placed in the electric buffet server in the dining room. The covers are put on, and the food is ready to serve at once, or an hour or two later. Because the electric heat will never heat the water too much, the food in the casseroles cannot burn and will not cook as it would on the ordinary chafing dish or hot plate.

Cleaning

The casseroles of the server are of the highest grade porcelain, and will give excellent service. The chromium covers and base of the server do not need polishing, or any abrasive powders, or liquids. The best way to keep the server in good condition is to dry it thoroughly after use and rub it briskly with a dry cloth. Keep it away from kitchen smoke and gases to protect its brilliant polish.

Use and Casserole Foods

A book "How to Give Buffet Suppers" by Emily Post is furnished free with each buffet server. Additional copies can be obtained for 10 cents in stamps, and on any large quantity for trade use, special prices will be quoted.

The Post Book is size 8 x 10⅝—twenty-four pages, with 15 illustrations, suggested buffet supper menus, 20 new recipes for buffet casserole dishes, and 50 suggested casserole foods.

We wish to call your particular attention to this Chase buffet server. We believe it is destined to be the most popular innovation of 1933-1934. It fills a real need, and it so happens that there is no other article on the market of the same kind.

Buffet meals are going to be popular this Winter. Chase national advertising will help make them so. Mrs. Post's word will influence many, and Chase chromium articles for buffet meals will help supply the demand.

The Chase Buffet Server is the most important piece for buffet meals. Display it, feature it in your window, on store tables. Set up a chromium buffet table and ride on this trend that will create Fall and Winter sales. Price, $40.00.

VIKING SAUCE BOWL No. 17046

VIKING SAUCE BOWL
No. 17046

This is one of the most beautiful designs we have ever made. It was designed by Von Nessen for mayonnaise, French dressing, gravy or fruit sauces. It is ideal for a wedding gift, attractively finished in polished chromium outside and satin chromium inside. The bowl handle is of black composition. Complete with ladle and tray to match. Price, $3.50 each.

LOTUS
SAUCE BOWL
No. 17045

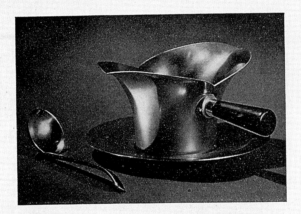

LOTUS SAUCE BOWL No. 17045

Like an open lotus blossom the lovely design of this bowl by Von Nessen is a delight to look at. For mayonnaise, gravy, or fruit sauces it is perfect, and blends with any design of silver. Finished in polished chromium outside and satin chromium inside. Black composition handle. Complete with ladle and tray to match. Price, $3.50 each.

CHEESE SERVER
No. 09009

There are certain good old rules for serving cheese. Cheese should be placed and cut on wood. It should be covered. And it should appear together with its crackers. This cheese server does all these things, and looks handsome besides. The tray is 14 inches in diameter and is built up from the center in three shallow steps on which crackers are arranged. Designed by the Gerths. Finished in lasting polished chromium. Prices: Cheese Server complete, $10.00; Tray only (No. 09010), $6.00 each.

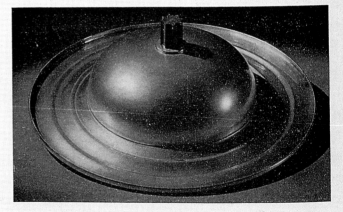

CHEESE SERVER No. 09009

SALAD BOWL No. 27006

SALAD BOWL
No. 27006

Wood is new and appropriate for salads. This modern bowl, spoon and fork, suggest the country garden, and the shining chromium shell dresses it up just enough to appear on the formal dinner table. Designed by Guild. Diameter 9¾ inches, height 4 inches, base 6¾ inches. Individually packed complete with wooden serving fork and spoon in gift box. Price, $6.00 each.

JAM SET
No. 90018

With metal cover and tray finished in satin copper, the hob nail glass jar is in a blush pink tone with a glass spoon to match. It is also made with chromium lid and tray with clear glass jar and spoon. Height 5¼ inches. Diameter 6⅜ inches. Packed in gift box. Price, $2.50 each.

JAM SET No. 90018

BREAKFAST SET   TOP NO. 26001   BOTTOM NO. 26003

BREAKFAST SET
No. 26003 complete   No. 26001 without tray

A three piece breakfast set of new semi-spherical design by the Gerths. The brilliance of the highly polished sugar bowl and creamer is set off by the black handles. An etched design decorates the tray. Dimensions: sugar bowl 4¼ inches high, 3¾ inches in diameter; creamer 3⅛ inches in diameter, 4⅞ inches long overall; tray 11⅜ inches long, 5 inches wide, ⅜ inch in depth. Finished in polished chromium. Prices: Set, $3.00 each; set without tray, $2.50 each.

HOT SERVICE COVER No. 90006-7

HOT SERVICE COVER
No. 90006-7

A very useful accessory for hot plates. Designed by the Gerths, it is finished in polished chromium with a catalin handle. Available in two sizes—No. 90006, 7¼ inches diameter, height 2¾ inches. Price, $3.00 each. No. 90007, diameter 8½ inches, height 3¼ inches. Price, $3.50 each.

COASTER SET
No. 11261

Coasters that will not stick to the glass. They may be had in satin copper or polished chromium. Attractively boxed in sets of four as illustrated. Price, $1.00 per set. Also sold one dozen to a box. (No. 11262) Price, $3.00 per dozen.

COASTER SET No. 11261

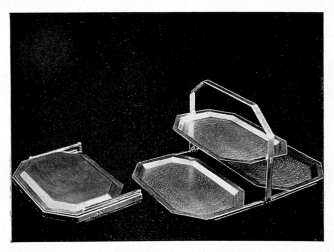

TRIPLE TRAY No. 09001

TRIPLE TRAY
No. 09001

This will hold a variety of cakes or sandwiches and take little space on the table. It is collapsible and can be easily put away in a drawer when not in use. Size (folded up) 7½ inches by 11 inches. Finished in polished chromium. Packed in attractive gift box. Price, $6.00 each.

TRAY No. NS-287

TRAY
No. NS-287

A sturdy tray in polished or satin copper or polished chromium, to hold many glasses, 12 inches diameter, with a small beaded flange about ¾ inch high. Designed by Von Nessen. Individually packed. Price for copper finishes, $3.00 each. Price for chromium, $4.00 each.

INDIVIDUAL CANAPÉ PLATE
No. 27001

With this smart looking canapé plate you can hold a cocktail, a canapé and a cigarette in one hand and shake hands with the other. The tray has a rimmed circle in it to hold the glass from sliding around. Shining chromium accentuates the beauty of its simple lines. Exclusive of its wing shaped handle, the tray measures 6¼ inches in diameter. Designed by Guild. Packed six to a gift box. Price, $1.00 each.

INDIVIDUAL CANAPÉ PLATE No. 27001

TIFFIN TRAY No. 17027

TIFFIN TRAY
No. 17027

An unusual serving tray that holds a lot without crowding. It will hold the Diplomat coffee set and four demitasse cups easily. Designed by Von Nessen. Length 18 inches, width 12 inches. In beautiful polished chromium, satin copper or polished copper with black handles. Price, $7.50 each.

SERVING TRAY No. 09002

SERVING TRAY
No. 09002

A large round tray with plenty of room for all sorts of plates and glasses, and a huge help in serving refreshments or buffet meals. Diameter of tray is 18 inches. Finished in lustrous satin copper, polished copper, or polished chromium. Individually boxed. Price, $6.00 each.

ROUND TRAY
No. 09011

A simple inexpensive server ideally adapted to the bridge foursome. It is 8¾ inches in diameter and has an attractive corrugated edge ⅝ inch high. Finished in highly polished copper or chromium. Packed one in a gift box. Prices: copper, 50c each; chromium, 60c each.

ROUND TRAY No. 09011

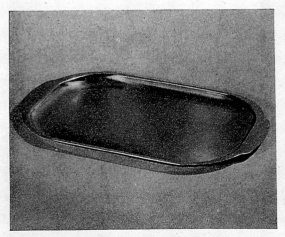

INFORMAL SERVING TRAY No. 09012

INFORMAL
SERVING TRAY
No. 09012

The combination of an oval exterior and an oblong interior with rounded corners gives this comparatively small 15 inch overall tray much more carrying room than is apparent. The recessed bottom provides a deep ridge one-half inch high which prevents glasses from sliding over the edge. Finished in gleaming polished chromium or polished copper. Price, $2.00 each.

CHASE "QUIET POOL" DESIGN

The sandwich plate, service plates, cold meat platter and bread tray illustrated below are all of the new Chase "Quiet Pool" design by Guild. "A pebble dropped in a still pool of water creates concentric circles." This is the theme of the design of these new plates and platters. The finish is polished chromium and the hair line circles are sharply etched through the chromium to the pure metal so that the effect is of pure gold lines against the silvery chromium. The simplicity of this design assures harmony with other table pieces. The different plates and trays can be displayed together and sold separately, and give any table a great brilliance and smartness.

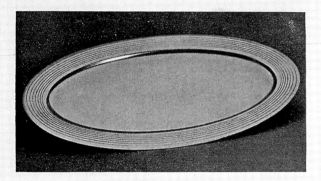

BREAD TRAY
No. 27005

13½ inches long, 8 inches wide. Price, $3.50 each.

COLD MEAT PLATTER
No. 27004

15 inches long, 9½ inches wide. Price, $4.00 each.

SANDWICH PLATE
No. 27003   13 inches in diameter.

Polished copper or chromium. Price, $4.00 each.

SERVICE PLATE
No. 27002

10½ inches in diameter. Price, $3.00 each.

"ARCHITEX" ADJUSTABLE CENTERPIECE

ARCHITEX ADJUSTABLE CENTERPIECE No. 27012

Here is a decorative centerpiece for the dinner table which can be varied in twenty different ways. You can be your own table architect, and build your flowers and candles into the shape and design you choose. The Architex centerpiece can be made large and spread out for the formal dinner, or small, round and friendly for the small dinner. It can be modernistic in arrangement, or conventional and reserved.

Description

The centerpiece consists of ten separate pieces; four candlesticks, four quartercircle boxes, and two rectangular boxes. The boxes are raised slightly from the table on small black legs, and the decorative lines and base moulding of each box is identical so that being placed close together they seem all one piece.

Flower Holder

Each box is furnished with a wire flower holder, which fits firmly in the box and holds the flowers easily in either a formal or spray arrangement.

HOW IT LOOKS WITH FLOWERS AND CANDLES

Candles

Colored candles can be made an important part of any table color scheme. For the four candle boxes of the Architex centerpiece you can use four candles of the same color, or two pairs of different colors. For example, four green candles, or two mahogany and and two tan or pink.

Low Flowers

The real smartness of the Architex centerpiece comes in using small or low flowers. Keep the flower arrangement low; first, because it is easy to see your neighbors across the table and talk with them. Second, because it is new and different from the usual flower arrangement.

Important Sales Note

One reason this centerpiece will appeal to many customers is that it uses short stemmed flowers which are cheap! Short stemmed roses, carnations and other flowers are at bargain prices at the florists. Here is a centerpiece container that can use them to advantage.

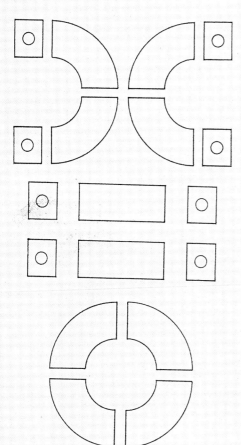

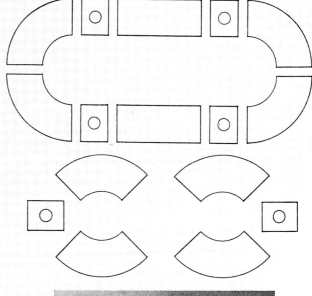

The handy wire device shown in the photograph holds the flowers in any desired position.

Arrangement of Boxes

We show above five of the different ways to arrange this "Architex" centerpiece. Many other ways can be worked out to suit individual tastes.

Suggested Flower Arrangements

1. Carnations (Try filling each box with one color only.) (Example: red, white, red, white, using dark blue candles.)
2. Narcissus and grape Hyacinth, and white candles.
3. English daisy, dark pink candles.
4. Pansies, mixed or single colors.
5. Purple Violets—steel blue candles.
6. Red and yellow Wallflower, dark red candles.
7. Pink and lavender Phlox—deep pink candles.
8. Pompon white Chrysanthemums, red candles.
9. Pompon pink Chrysanthemums, light blue candles.
10. Bachelors Buttons and white Candytuft in alternate diagonal stripes, red candles.

Other good flowers to use are snapdragon, calendula, zinnia, nasturtium, sweet peas. All berries—such as bittersweet, etc. with or without cut ivy ends can also be used.

Use short stemmed flowers. Cut the stems slanting and keep in a cool place until ready to use on the table. Flowers will last longer if placed in a cool pantry at night.

Remember that in the Architex centerpiece the flowers and candles must be considered together as one color scheme. Use white candles, of course, at anytime, but fascinating arrangements of color can be worked out with colored candles, colored tablecloths, and flowers, as well as by varying the arrangement of the Architex pieces themselves.

Prices: complete set of ten pieces (27012) $20.00; circular centerpiece only (27008) $2.00 each; rectangular centerpiece only (27009) $2.00 each; candlestick only (27007) $2.00 each.

TAUREX CANDLESTICKS No. 24004 AND No. 24003

TAUREX CANDLESTICKS
No. 24003   No. 24004

A reasonably priced candlestick by Von Nessen, designed to hold two candles in the new smart even and uneven arrangement. For a suggestion, display them with one blue and one green candle. Finished in polished chromium or polished copper. Packed one in a gift box. The uneven candle holder is 9¾ inches high. The even candle holder is 7⅛ inches high. Price, $3.00 each.

SUNDAY SUPPER CANDLE HOLDERS
No. 24002

Designed to fit into any scheme of decoration and excellent to use in groups on the dining table. They are low and easy to look over. They are well balanced and look exceptionally well with tall candles. Height 1¾ inches, diameter 3⅜ inches. Finished in black nickel; polished copper; satin brass or satin nickel. A set of four in attractive gift box. Price, $1.00 per set.

SUNDAY SUPPER CANDLE HOLDER No. 24002

DISC CANDLESTICKS No. 24005

DISC CANDLESTICKS
No. 24005

Here is how a good designer can combine discs with a sphere. This smart candlestick holds two candles. The flat polished surfaces reflect the lights and colors of the dinner table. These candlesticks are exceptionally good looking with tall dark navy blue candles. Designed by the Gerths. Height 4¾ inches, width 8½ inches. Finished in polished chromium, satin copper or polished copper. Price, $4.00 each.

DIPLOMAT COFFEE SET WITH TRAY

COFFEE SET No. 17029   TRAY No. 17030

Here is an aid to brilliant entertaining. Of marked individuality in the design by Von Nessen, the coffee pot, sugar and creamer come in polished chromium, or polished copper with white tinned lining inside. The handles and knobs are of composition in a highly polished black finish. Dimensions: coffee pot, diameter 2⅜ inches, height over-all 8 inches; sugar bowl, diameter 2⅜ inches, height over-all 4 inches; creamer, diameter 2⅜ inches, height 2¾ inches. The black mirror-like finish of the tray affords a striking contrast. The rolled edge of the tray is available in chromium or polished copper. Diameter of tray 10 inches. Coffee Set: Price, $15.00. Tray: Price, $5.00 each.

TABLE BELLS

13002 BRITTANY   13004 CUCKOO
13003 RONDO   13005 APOLLO

No. 13002

No. 13003

No. 13004

No. 13005

Four very striking table bells with a pleasant ring and attractive appearance. Made of brass and finished in all polished brass, or with chromium bells and black nickel handles. "Rondo" and "Apollo," the tallest bells, are 4 inches high. May be ordered in assortments of designs and finishes in dozen lots. One packed to a gift box. Price, $1.00 each.

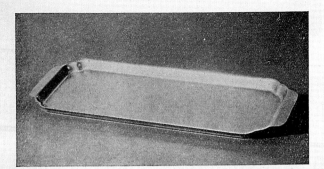

COCKTAIL TRAY No. 09013

COCKTAIL TRAY
No. 09013

This simple cocktail tray is ideal for use with cocktail cups, No. 26002, but may be used equally as well with other cocktail service pieces. It comes individually packed in either polished chromium, or polished copper finish. Over-all dimensions $15\frac{7}{8}$ inches long, $5\frac{3}{8}$ inches wide. Price $2.00 each.

COCKTAIL SHAKER
No. 90034

Entirely modern in its appearance, it retains the usefulness of old-fashioned shakers. The top is fitted with a sleeve which fits snugly into the pouring lip when shaking to prevent leaking or spilling of contents. A strainer is also provided to hold back the mint, lemon or other solids. Finished in bright chromium with black enamel rings at top and bottom. Height $11\frac{1}{2}$ inches; diameter $3\frac{3}{4}$ inches. Individually packed in gift box. Price, $4.00 each.

COCKTAIL SHAKER No. 90034

COCKTAIL CUP No. 26002

COCKTAIL CUP
No. 26002

Simplicity is an outstanding feature in the design of this distinctive cocktail cup, but it is the simplicity of line and decoration that suggests sophistication and good taste. It is 2 inches high, $2\frac{3}{4}$ inches in diameter and is finished in polished chromium outside and satin chromium inside. Price, 50c each.

NIBLICK SWIZZLERS
No. 90037

These chromium plated Niblick Swizzlers by Guild are new and better than spoons for mixing iced drinks. The niblick blade and round slender 7⅜ inch handle slide down through the ice to the bottom of the glass without swelling the liquid over the glass edge. Packed set of four to a box. Price, 50c per set.

Swizzlers No. 90037

Candy Dish No. 90011

CANDY DISH
No. 90011

A candy dish with a three-compartment glass liner fitted into a well-shaped holder. The etched cover has a fruit cluster knob for a handle finished the same as the dish holder. Designed by the Gerths. Made in the following finishes: black nickel bottom, satin nickel top; satin copper bottom, satin brass top; all satin brass; all satin copper. Diameter 7 inches; height 3¼ inches. Price, $1.00 each.

CONFECTION BOWL
No. 90027

A confection bowl designed with good taste and character. May be had in a combination of satin copper and black glass, or polished chromium and black glass. Both finishes harmonize with serving accessories, and the inlaid enamel colors on the flange give it a well dressed appearance. The bowl is 4 inches in diameter and 2 inches deep. Packed individually in gift box. Price, 75c each.

Confection Bowl No. 90027

IMPERIAL BOWL No. 15003

IMPERIAL BOWL
No. 15003

This graceful fruit or flower bowl is made of satin copper with a satin silver lining and black nickel base, or polished chromium with satin silver lining and black nickel base. The piece stands 4 inches high and is 8½ inches in diameter. Packed in attractive gift box. Prices: copper or chromium finish, $6.00 each.

TROPHY VASE No. 03005

TROPHY VASE
No. 03005

Tall and tapered toward the base similar to the traditional loving cup. The graceful flared top will accommodate large bouquets. Diameter of base 3 inches. Height 9 inches. In three finishes: triangle metal (golden) satin finish, chromium, and black nickel. Price, $3.50 each.

CALYX VASE
No. 03007-8

This smartly flared vase has a simplicity of design that is refreshing. Either the polished copper or the polished chromium assures a graceful container for cut flowers. It is available in two convenient sizes. The small size (No. 03007) is 6½ inches high. Prices: polished copper, $1.00 each; chromium, $1.50 each. The large size (No. 03008) is 7½ inches high. Prices: polished copper, $1.75 each; chromium, $2.00 each.

No. 03007   No. 03008
CALYX VASE

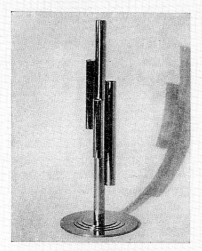

FOUR TUBE BUD HOLDER No. 11230

FOUR TUBE
BUD HOLDER
No. 11230

A useful, decorative holder, cleverly combining brass and copper—the center tube is of copper supplemented by brass cluster tubes. The steps of the base are alternate brass and copper. Also available in all polished chromium. Height 8¼ inches, diameter 3½ inches. Individually packed. Price: combination brass and copper or chromium, $1.00 each.

VICTORIAN VASE
No. 03006

This smart combination of a sphere with a tubular shaped top creates a quaint setting for flowers. Height 6⅜ inches. Finished in polished copper. Packed individually in attractive gift box. Price, $1.50 each.

VICTORIAN VASE No. 03006

RING VASE No. 17039

RING VASE
No. 17039

Four rings of colorful enamel and a flared top stress the simplicity and beauty of this vase for tall flowers by Walter Von Nessen. Height 9½ inches. Diameter 4 inches. Finished in chromium with black rings, or golden triangle metal with rings of lapis blue. One to a gift box. Prices: for chromium, $3.00 each; golden triangle metal, $2.50 each.

DISPLAY YOUR BEER ARTICLES IN SETS

Chase Beer Pitchers, beer mugs, trays and pretzel bowls are not shipped or sold to the trade in sets. There are so many different combinations that can be made of pieces in various designs and finishes that we believe that you would rather make up your own sets.

Sets Sell More Volume

It is an advantage to sell by the set. The beer mugs help sell the pitcher, and both help sell the tray and bowl. We have found that more merchandise will be sold if the articles are displayed and specially priced as a set.

Sell Separately Also

Of course, you will want to sell the different pieces separately, but we believe the set idea will sell more goods for you.

Select Your Combinations

For this reason we are illustrating below a few combinations which you can buy separately and display together. Countless other sets can be combined from the individual pieces shown on the following pages, which you can select as you like. The wide range of prices possible through various combinations will help sales materially.

A "HER AND HIM" SET

A ROMAN FEAST-DAY SET

A POPULAR PRICED SET

A CHESHIRE MUG SET

BACCHUS GOBLET
No. 90032

A design by the Gerths, suggestive of the wine feasts of Roman days. This design, coupled with its 18 ounce capacity, makes the Bacchus Goblet a favorite. It's a grand glass to toast with! Height 6 inches, diameter 3 inches. Polished copper or chromium with tinned lining. Individually packed. Price, $1.50 each.

BEER MUG
No. 90042

An inexpensive but very practical copper mug. Shaped like a miniature keg, it has a rolled edge and sturdy seamless handle. Fine for outdoor drinking fountain and well use. It is finished in polished copper or chromium with tinned lining. 4 inches high; 4¾ inches wide; capacity approximately 15 ounces. Prices: copper, 39c each; chromium, 50c each.

CHESHIRE MUG
No. 90031

Here's a tankard that smacks of Old New England and the "Cheshire Cheese" tap room. Notice the unique semi-circular handle and the smooth rolled edge. A choice of finishes is offered; polished chromium, or polished copper with brass handle and tinned lining. Designed by the Gerths. 4 inches high, 3¼ inches in diameter. Capacity 18 ounces. Price, $1.00 each.

CHESHIRE MUG No. 90031

PRETZEL BOWL
No. 15004

The charm of this pretzel bowl is in its plain graceful simplicity. It is 7 inches in diameter at the top with a depth of 2⅝ inches and will hold quite a supply of pretzels. The base is 3 inches in diameter. Finished in polished copper or polished chromium. Price, $2.00 each.

BACCHUS PITCHER
No. 90036

Originated for use with Bacchus Goblets, this pitcher has the same attractive thumb-print design. The long, tapering, pouring lip and the unusual shape of the handle add distinctiveness. Height 10¼ inches, width 8¾ inches, capacity three pints. Finished in either polished copper or polished chromium. Prices: copper, $5.00 each; chromium, $6.00 each.

PRETZELMAN No. 90038

PRETZELMAN
No. 90038

This high-stepping, jolly pretzelman holds a generous supply of pretzels above the beer glasses below. He was designed by Guild to be equally adept at carrying doughnuts or cookies with holes in them. He stands 18 inches high and is finished in gleaming copper or chromium. Prices: copper, $1.00 each; chromium, $1.75 each.

DEVONSHIRE
PITCHER

No. 90025

An old-but-new pitcher finished in either polished copper or chromium with a white tinned lining. This roomy pitcher holds two quarts. Packed one to a gift box. Prices: polished copper, $3.00 each; chromium, $3.50 each.

SALEM
WATER PITCHER

No. 90004

Colonial style pitcher in polished copper with white tinned lining. Designed by Gerth and Gerth. Capacity, two quarts. Height 9¾ inches, width 7⅜ inches. Individually packed in gift box. Price, $5.00 each.

TAVERN PITCHER

No. 17026

Graceful lines characterize this pitcher designed by Von Nessen. Finished in polished copper with white tinned lining and polished brass handle. Capacity, three pints. Height 10¼ inches, width 8¾ inches. Packed in individual boxes. Price, $6.00 each.

TAVERN PITCHER No. 17026

FRENCH WATERING CAN
No. 05001

An attractive European type watering can that conjures up a picture of a cool French garden. It has a beautiful long spout curving at the end and a graceful yet sturdy handle. And it holds almost a gallon. Made in a pleasing combination of polished copper and brass. 8¼ inches high, 23 inches from handle to tip of spout. Individually packed. Price, $10.00 each.

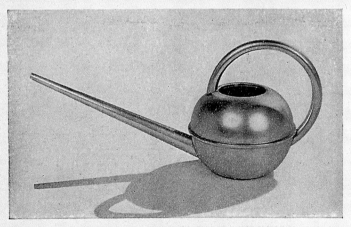

RAIN-BEAU WATERING CAN
No. 05002

Like a round gleaming copper ball with a brass handle arched over the top. Its long spout is very convenient in watering house plants. Holds one pint. Attractively packed one to a gift box. Price, $1.00 each.

RAIN-BEAU WATERING CAN No. 05002

PENDANT PLANT BOWL
No. 04004

An unusual design for a hanging flower bowl. The attractive ring design gives the appearance of the modern step-down effect. The chains are placed to keep the bowl hanging evenly. Depth of bowl 5½ inches, diameter 6¼ inches, height, including chain, 20 inches. Finished in polished brass; polished copper; and English bronze. Packed in a gift box. Price, $1.00 each.

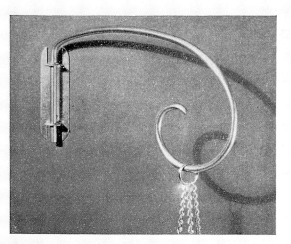

ROUND ROD
WALL BRACKET
No. 90029

This round rod wall bracket will support pendant flower bowls, bird cages and lanterns easily and gracefully. Also an excellent support for the Chase Binnacle Light (No. 25001) illustrated on page 36. Finished in satin brass, copper or English bronze. The arm length is 9½ inches and hinge length 4¾ inches. Price, 50c each.

MAGNO
GARDEN MARKER
No. 11108

A unique garden marker with a glass top that magnifies the lettering on the name card. 13 inches long; diameter of head, 1¾ inches. Head is green enameled on weather-resisting non-rustable brass. Price, 2 for 25c.

MAGNO GARDEN MARKER No. 11108

INDOOR FLOWER CULTIVATOR No. 11233

INDOOR FLOWER
CULTIVATOR
No. 11233

A combination rake and spade for loosening the earth in potted plants. Finished in combination polished brass and copper. Individually boxed. Price, 25c each.

RIBBED FLOWER POT
No. 04003

A large enough flower pot with a very different and attractive design. The close ribbed treatment is modern in feeling and yet harmonizes with old furnishings. And the graceful spread at the top catches any excess water when watering. Height 5⅜ inches. Finished in satin copper. One to a gift box. Price, $1.00 each.

RIBBED FLOWER POT No. 04003

FLOWER POT HOLDER No. 11155

FLOWER POT HOLDER
No. 11155

In a modern stepped down design, with saucer to match. May be had in polished brass or polished copper. Diameter 5¾ inches, height 4½ inches. Individually packed in attractive gift box. Price, $1.00 each.

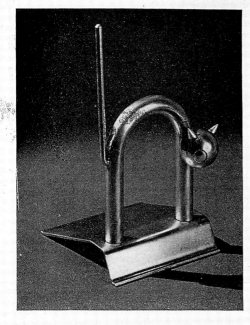

CAT DOOR STOP
No. 90035

Here's a door stop with no pretty pink flowers, no Dutch windmills, no little girls in long dresses. Here's a solid, handsome metal cat, dignified but humorous, that will hold your door open and stop draft slams. Combination polished brass and copper, or satin nickel and black. Height 8½ inches, width 4½ inches, depth 4¾ inches. Price, $1.50 each.

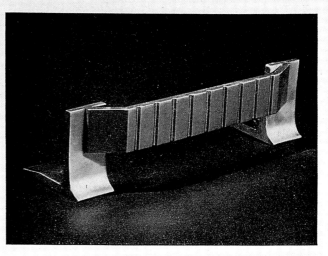

FOOT SCRAPER
No. 90033

This sturdy rust-proof footscraper will add dignity to the entrance of your home as well as help to preserve fine floor finishes. Solid brass construction—built for a lifetime of service. Length 7 inches, height 2 inches. Individually packed in box complete with brass screws for attaching. Price, $1.50 each.

WEATHER VANE
No. 90030

This all-brass non-rusting weather vane will reach the peak of many well-kept homes this year. The graceful arrow pivots on a solid brass point enabling it to give years of service without impairing its sensitive efficiency. Height 12 inches; width 12 inches. Individually packed in box with brass screws for attaching. Price, $1.00 each.

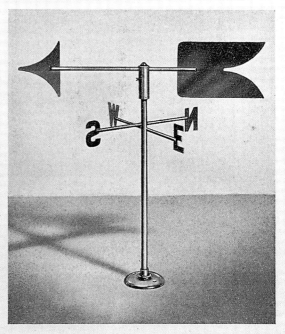

WEATHER VANE No. 90030

GLOW LAMP No. 01001

GLOW LAMP
No. 01001

Although this little lamp is particularly pleasing in a cozy setting, it is fine as a night light or for use in the sick room. The cone-shaped top fits well down over the bulb and can be tilted at any angle. The light is reflected in a soft glow. Height with bulb 8¼ inches over-all, width 6 inches. In polished copper or polished chromium or combination black and chromium. Prices: copper, $1.00 each; polished chromium, $1.50 each; black and chromium, $1.00 each.

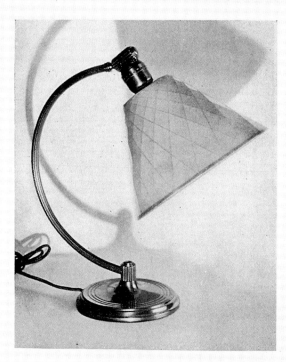

FLUTED BASE TABLE LAMP
No. 01005

Here is an unusual lamp that will harmonize with almost any period of decoration and yet be beautiful in itself. The light reflects from the polished chromium fluted sides of the base giving brilliant kaleidoscopic refractions. Height, 16 inches; diameter of shade, 12 inches. Finished in polished chromium and black. Price, packed in individual gift box complete with shade, $7.50 each.

DESK LAMP
No. 01003

An attractive lamp with a rare combination of dignity and usefulness. The lamp, swiveled on a sturdy semi-circular bracket, can be adjusted in nearly any desirable position. The shade is of very effective design in an old ivory color. Just the thing for the writing desk or reading table. Height 14½ inches, diameter 5¾ inches. Finished in English bronze or polished chromium. Price, $3.00 each.

CONSTELLATION LAMP
No. 17048

Here is one of the most perfect small lamps we have
ever made. For the telephone table, a desk, or small
occasional table, it is exactly right. The trim modern
lines give it a sense of freshness and novelty that is
very attractive. The top tilts in any direction to shade
the frosted globe. Designed by Von Nessen. Finished in polished chromium, or copper, or antique
English bronze. Height 8½ inches, diameter 7½
inches. Price, $2.00 each.

CONSTELLATION LAMP No. 17048

CIRCLE LAMP
No. 01004

The graceful lines and exquisite finish of this
modern lamp combine with the practical use for
which it was designed. The shade works on a swivel
which can be adjusted to any convenient angle for
reading. It is ideal for use on an end table. Size; 14
inches high, 12 inches wide. Finished in polished
chromium or English bronze. Complete with harmonizing shade. Price, $5.00 each.

SHIP AHOY LIGHT
No. 01006

The theme of the old ship's lantern base of
highly polished brass and colored globe is fully
carried out in the smart mariner's shade. It is perfect
for your porch, guest room, or son's room. The
over-all height is 10½ inches and the lantern is provided with either red or green globe. Individual
switches are provided for the base light and the
upper light. Price, $2.00 each.

REEDED LAMP No. 01009

REEDED LAMP

No. 01009

A beautiful design, sparkling and smart, that blends equally well in old-fashioned and modern surroundings. The reeded pattern of the lamp standard is carried out in the parchment shade which is accordion pleated. The lamp is finished in polished copper, or white enamel. Height 10¾ inches, base 4 inches. Price, $1.50 each

CENTURY LAMP

No. 01008

An up-to-date looking lamp and not too modernistic to fit in any room. The base is finished in either black or white enamel with two chromium panels. The natural parchment shade, with a sparsely stippled effect and two half-inch black bands bordered with silver is in harmony with the base. Height 15 inches. Price, $6.00 each.

TANKARD LAMP

No. 01007

This barrel beer mug converted into a lamp makes a timely debut for use at 3.2 parties and for decorating private bars. It is also well suited for sun rooms, or used as a pair on a man's bedroom bureau. Height, 11 inches. The base is finished in highly polished copper and the parchment shade is tinted a faint copper hue. Price, $1.00 each.

BALL LAMP No. 11235

BALL LAMP
No. 11235

A unique design by the Gerths in a table lamp that has definite appeal. The large circular parchment shade is decorated with parallel lines in accord with the design of the lamp body. Made in all polished chromium or a combination of polished brass base and polished copper ball. Height over-all, 15 inches. Packed individually. Price, $7.50 each, complete.

CONSOLE LAMP
No. 27010

A beautiful lamp of polished chromium designed by Lurelle Guild. The highly polished base, mirror-like, reflects the colors of the room, and while modern in design, it harmonizes quietly with any style of decoration. (Display it next to color, such as a red book, or brightly colored flowers, which will reflect in the polished lamp side.) The lamp, in chromium, with its specially designed shade, is 17 inches over-all, base 5 inches. Price, $7.50 each.

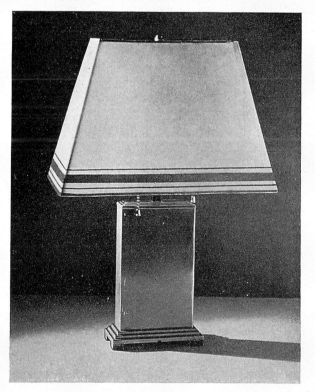

CONSOLE LAMP No. 27010

Bomb Flashlight No. 22001

"BOMB" FLASHLIGHT

No. 22001

A new type flashlight that will stand by itself, slip over the wrist or hang from a hook. Neat and compact; fits the coat pocket, takes little space in a car pocket. Diameter 3½ inches, 1¾ inches thick. Finished in polished nickel and packed separately in an illustrated box as shown or in an attractive 3-color counter display container that holds six lights. Complete with batteries and bulbs. Price, $1.00 each.

"AIRALITE"

No. 22003

A smart and handy companion to the powder compact; a small vest pocket flashlight. It measures but 2 x 2½ inches. Airalite has the candlepower and switch equipment of a much larger flashlight. It hangs on a hook or stands on its own base. Finished in polished nickel with colored enamel inlays to give it smartness and beauty. Takes a standard pen-light battery. Has unbreakable lens. Packed in individual gift box, or six Airalites to a display card designed for window or show case use. Complete with batteries and bulbs. Price, 75c each.

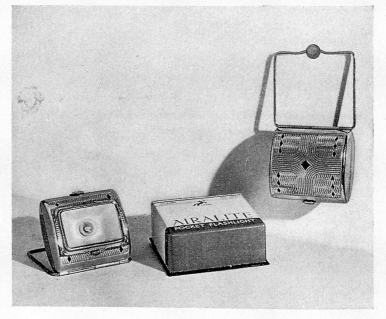

Airalite No. 22003

COLONEL LIGHT
No. 27013

This militant "Colonel" will delight the child who is fortunate enough to own it. The Colonel's head is an electric light bulb, and the tall Cossack hat is a shade that can be tilted at a cocky angle to shade the light from the child's bed. The Colonel's coat is flashing red with bright yellow buttons. Consider selling a pair for a child's bureau. Wired complete for plugging into regular house circuit. Height 9⅜ inches, base diameter 4 inches. Price, $2.00 each.

COLONEL LIGHT No. 27013

BINNACLE LIGHT No. 25002

BINNACLE LIGHTS
No. 25001-2

A small, brass finished lamp in a nautical design, either complete with flashlight batteries or wired for electricity, and complete with bulb. It gives sufficient illumination for a porch or hall. Equipped with frosted glass globe. It may be carried in the hand, hung on a hook, or set on the table. Height 5½ inches, diameter 3¼ inches. Individually packed in gift box. No. 25001 takes two intermediate size batteries. Price, $1.00 each. No. 25002 operates from electrical outlet. Price, 1.00 each.

VANITY MIRROR No. 90043

VANITY MIRROR
No. 90043

Heavily chrome plated and buffed to perfection, this dainty metal vanity mirror has an unusually bright reflecting surface—impervious to moisture and unbreakable. The back is enameled in colors with a contrasting enameled etched design. Diameter 2⅜ inches. Price, 25c each.

HANDY DRYER
No. 11232

A practical and convenient dryer made of brass, finished in beautiful pastel shades of blue, green, old rose and orchid. Furnished on cards as illustrated, one dozen assorted colors to a box. Price, 25c per card. No. 90003 packed four to a gift box, all one color. Price, $1.00 per box.

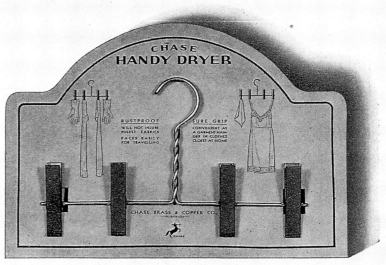

HANDY DRYER No. 11232

SEWPACT
No. 90026

A sewing compact with an assortment of pin sizes, a card of black, white, tan and brown thread. A pair of scissors, a thimble and a few needles. Width 2¼ inches, length 3¼ inches, thickness ¾ inch. Fits a woman's handbag, or overnight bag. Convenient to carry in car pocket. Practical for use at home and indispensable for the traveler. Made of brass and finished in satin brass, or nickel with a floral inlay of assorted colors on the cover. Packed in gift box. Price, $1.00 each.

SEWPACT No. 90026

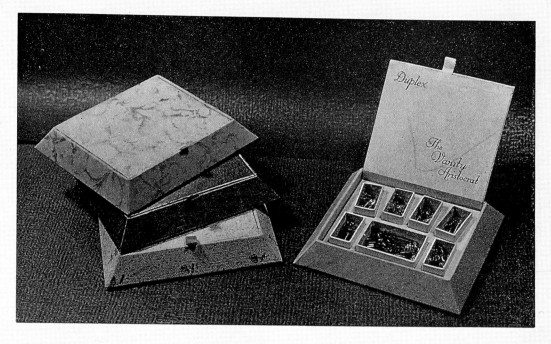

THE VANITY ARISTOCRAT

No. 1002A

This Duplex safety pin set should have a place on every dressing table. It occupies but little space, and is an invaluable convenience. From the tiny size 00 (both in nickel and gold plate) to size 2, these handy pins are sorted according to size and finish into seven individual compartments. The box itself, measuring 4⅞ x 5¼ inches, is finished in a choice of coverings to harmonize with any surroundings—blue, green, pink or light flowered design. It may be refilled with Duplex safety pins or used as a container for other articles if desired. Price, 50 cents each.

DUPLEX PINPACKS

No. 1001 AND No. 1001A

Here is a modern safety pin package that belongs in a woman's handbag with her lipstick, powder and mirror. Neatly packed in the chic folding container are twelve Duplex safety pins of rust-proof Chase brass. No. 1001 Pinpacks are boxed in lots of twelve in solid sizes. No. 1001A is an attractive display cabinet containing three dozen Pinpacks of assorted sizes: 00, 0, 1, 2, 2½ and 3. All pins are finished in nickel. Sizes 00 and 0 may also be obtained gold plated. Price, Duplex Pinpacks, 10 cents each.

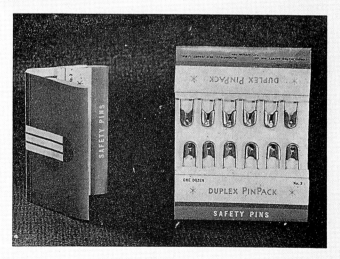

DUPLEX PINPACK No. 1001

CHASE

MIRROR TOP BOX

No. 21003

An exquisitely chaste design for a powder box with a handy mirror inside the top. The circular box is gracefully flared and is perfect for the dressing table. Designed by Reimann and finished in lustrous satin silver. The diameter is 5¾ inches and the depth, 2 inches. Price, individually packed in gift box, $1.50 each.

OCCASIONAL BOX

No. 90002

A dainty little box, made of brass finished in black, blue, rose, green or orchid enamel, trimmed with polished nickel. Comes with a glass lining. Designed by the Gerths. Diameter 4½ inches, height 2¼ inches plus knob. Individually boxed. Price, $1.00 each.

OCCASIONAL BOX No. 90002

Page 38

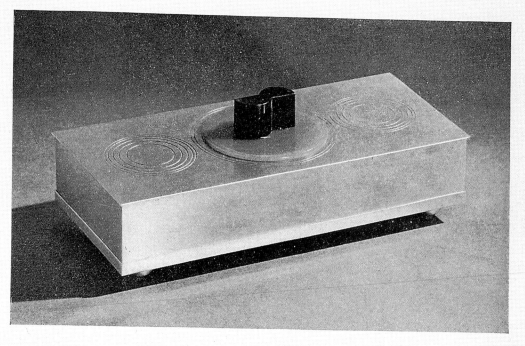

THE ROLLAROUND

No. 841

A neat modern cigarette box, mounted on four large ball bearings. It can easily be rolled across the table without scratching or marring the surface. The box is lined throughout with a wood veneer humidor, divided into three compartments, and will hold sixty cigarettes.

The top is decoratively etched with concentric circles and a splash of color is added in the unique red and black Bakelite handle. The Rollaround is finished in lustrous satin nickel. By the Gerths. Size: 7 inches long, 3 inches wide, 1¼ inches high. Price, $2.00 each.

CONNOISSEUR

No. 842

Simple in both line and finish, this rectangular cigarette box blends without difficulty into almost any surroundings. It is that sort of simple design that looks quality and taste. The cover is decorated in the modern manner with hair-line geometric etchings. Inside, the box is divided into three separate wooden lined compartments, each of sufficient size to accommodate twenty cigarettes. The Connoisseur is finished in soft, satin copper or satin nickel. By the Gerths. It is 7 inches long, 3 inches wide and 1¼ inches high. Price, $1.00 each.

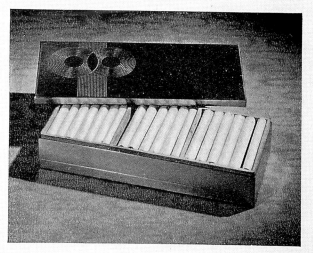

CONNOISSEUR No. 842

ROUNDABOUT ASH TRAY
No. 821

This ash tray makes an unusually striking effect because the light reflects around the tray from the highly polished ridges. It is 5¼ inches in diameter and lined with glass. Finished in satin brass outside and jade inside or satin nickel and black inside. Price, neatly packed, 25c each.

ARISTOCRAT ASH TRAY
No. 835

This ash tray makes use of the striking motifs of modern architecture. Strong horizontal lines and vertical lines and reflecting flat surfaces are used. The receptacle is 1 inch deep and 4 inches in diameter. Over-all width, 5½ inches. Polished chromium or polished copper. Price, $1.00 each.

TIP TILT ASH TRAY
No. 819

A convenient ash tray 3¾ inches in diameter. The ashes are deposited by tilting the balanced disc on top. Available in polished nickel with either a black or red stripe, and satin brass with black stripe. Price, individually packed in gift box, 25c each.

THE "FOURSOME"
ASH RECEIVER SET
No. 844

These individual bowl-shaped trays are very practical as well as lovely in shape. Each tray has ample capacity, and is supported by three sturdy legs. Finished in polished chromium that is easily and quickly cleaned. Per set of 4 trays, $1.00.

SMOKESTACK

No. 831

Modern in design, and useful on the bridge table. This cigarette container holds twenty cigarettes in a neat stack. Consider placing one at each place for the informal supper table. Bright chromium, English bronze, or black nickel finish. Over-all dimensions 3¾ inches long, 2¼ inches wide, 2 inches high. Price, $1.00 each.

SMOKESTACK No. 831

CIGARETTE SERVER AND ASH TRAY No. 824

CIGARETTE SERVER AND ASH TRAY

No. 824

A combination ash tray and cigarette server that is especially shaped to fit end tables or narrow smokers' cabinets. The ash tray is of black glass 8 inches long and 4 inches wide, with three rests. The cigarette server is finished in polished nickel with either black, red, or green enamel trim. Price, 75c each.

HUMPTY DUMP ASH TRAY

No. 500

A neat appearing and very practical ash tray from which the ashes can easily be removed. Revolving disc, easily moved by ornamental post, deposits ashes in glass receptacle. Polished copper and orange glass or golden triangle metal and black glass. Price, 50c each.

HUMPTY DUMP ASH TRAY No. 500

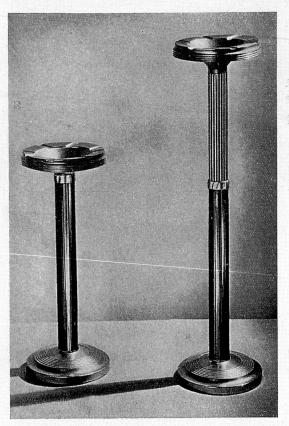

HI-LO SMOKER'S STAND No. 836

HI-LO SMOKERS' STAND

No. 836

This smoke stand won't let cigarettes smolder and smoke. The upper half of the tube telescopes into the lower half. A few turns of the ring centered on the tube holds the tray at the desired height. To empty out ashes, separate the telescopic tubes and remove cap on bottom of upper tube. It is packed in a compact box disassembled in four parts; the base, two tubes, and the ash receiver. Finished in English bronze or combination polished chromium and red or black enamel. Height adjustable from 16½ inches to 25½ inches. Price, $1.75 each.

ECLIPSE ASH TRAY

No. 809

Ingeniously located spring holds cover in either open or closed position. When lighted cigarette or cigar end is dropped, cover can be closed and no odor escapes. Finished in polished brass and black enamel with red stripes; green, red or ivory enamel with black stripe. Price, 75c each.

ECLIPSE ASH TRAY No. 809

NOB-TOP ASH TRAY No. 810

NOB-TOP ASH TRAY
No. 810

An ash tray of generous size—6½ inches in diameter with a knob for carrying. Finished in chromium with a colored knob to match the inlaid red, green, tortoise shell or black enamel on the tray. Price, 75c each.

PENTAD ASH RECEIVERS
No. 840

Brilliantly finished in gleaming chromium, a set of these individual ash trays is both attractive and useful for the bridge foursome. Although they are big enough to hold plenty of ashes, they are not clumsy or top heavy. Neatly packed nests of four trays. Price, $1.00 each.

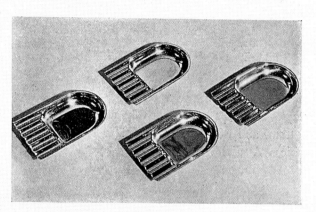

PENTAD ASH RECEIVER No. 840

FLUTED ASH TRAYS No. 17040

FLUTED ASH TRAYS
No. 17040

A new and extremely practical ash tray set designed by Von Nessen. The decorative fluted edge is designed to hold a cigarette regardless of the direction from which the tray is approached. The trays are 4 inches in diameter and are finished in lustrous satin chromium, black nickel or English bronze. Neatly packed, nest of four trays. Price, $1.00 each.

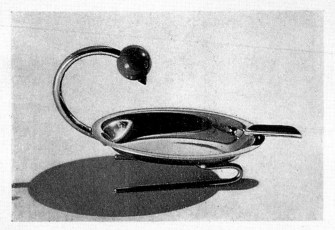

SWAN ASH TRAY No. 837

SWAN ASH TRAY
No. 837

So different than the usual ash tray designs that it will steal the conversation at any bridge table. The long legs with their reverse bend, the red head and large, round, black eyes are cheerful reminders to "deposit ashes here." Polished chromium finish. Height 3 inches, width 5½ inches. Price, $1.00 each.

COMPACT
CIGARETTE SERVER
No. 822

A cigarette server topped with a set of four ash trays. The trays are attractively engraved on the bottom, and of convenient size for use on card tables. Available in black, white, tortoise shell, or jade enamel with cover and ash trays of polished chromium. Price, $1.00 each.

COMPACT CIGARETTE SERVER No. 822

AUTOMATIC TABLE LIGHTER No. 825

AUTOMATIC
TABLE LIGHTER
No. 825

This decorative table lighter lights by just pressing the button conveniently located on the side of the lighter. When not in use, the mechanism is concealed under the highly polished chromium cover which gives a neat and trim appearance to the lighter. The finishes are chromium with either black, red, green, white, jade or tortoise shell enamel. It is 3¼ inches high and 1½ inches wide. Price, $1.00 each.

FOUR PIECE SMOKERS' SET
No. 823

Here is an unusual value. It consists of an attractive tray 11 inches long and 5 inches wide with a modern engine-turned design on the bottom. Also a cigarette server with ample room for forty cigarettes and two ash trays. The ash trays are ideal for use on a small stand or bridge table as the dome shape prevents ashes from being accidently blown or brushed off; and they can be easily taken apart and cleaned. The set is finished in English bronze; or polished nickel with either black, red or green enamel trim. Price, $1.00 each.

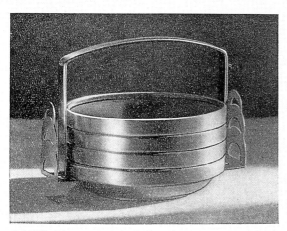

MATCH-PACK ASH TRAY
No. 820

This set of ash trays and holder is available in modernistic black and satin nickel with the trays lined in white. Also satin brass and English bronze with the trays lined in jade. Decorative clips at each side are arranged to hold book matches. Price, $1.00 each.

CROWN ASH TRAY
No. 811

Man-size ash tray with dumping feature which deposits ashes in concealed, glass-lined compartment. Opens easily for cleaning. Continuous rests around upper rim. Finished in polished chromium and red, green or black enamel. Packed in individual gift boxes. Price, $1.75 each.

CHASE CHROMIUM ˌ BRASS ˌ COPPER PRODUCTS

CIGARETTE SERVER AND ASH TRAY No. 806

CIGARETTE SERVER AND ASH TRAY

No. 806

A server that holds forty cigarettes, and lifts cigarettes into accessible position when button is released. Locks closed when pushed down. Large ash tray of heavy metal with three rests. All metal parts finished in polished chromium with red, green, white, tortoise shell, jade or black enamel. Packed in individual gift boxes. Price, $1.75 each.

AUTOMATIC LIGHTER AND TRAY

No. 828

A roomy ash tray 6½ inches in diameter equipped with an attractive automatic lighter. The lighter can easily be lifted out of the ash tray and used individually. The combination is ideal for card tables, informal suppers, and wherever groups gather. The lighter and tray are finished in chromium with a choice of black, white, tortoise shell, red or green enamel inlay. Price, $2.00 each.

AUTOMATIC LIGHTER AND TRAY No. 828

DE LUXE CIGARETTE SET No. 815

DE LUXE CIGARETTE SET

No. 815

This set consists of a large glass-lined tray, cigarette server with automatic release button, automatic lighter and four nested ash trays. All exposed metal parts finished in polished chromium in combination with red, green, white, jade, tortoise shell or black enamel. Packed in individual gift boxes. Price, $6.00 each.

"LAZY BOY" SMOKERS' STAND

No. 17031

An original and beautiful combination of ash stand and smokers' cabinet designed by Von Nessen. Dignified and serious enough for a man's office and yet handsome enough for the most luxurious living room. It is in keeping with either old or modern furniture and decoration. It has a roomy compartment for pipe, tobacco, cigars and cigarettes which is easily accessible by sliding open the top which pivots around the ash tray. The special composition top is durable as well as alcohol-proof. This insures a permanently neat and trim appearance. The base is heavily weighted to prevent tipping. The ash container runs the length of the corrugated tube and can be easily cleaned by lifting up the ash tray and tube. The spring attached to the cover of the ash tray keeps it tightly closed when not in use. This eliminates any odor from stale tobacco ashes. The Lazy Boy is available in two finishes: English bronze, or a combination of black and satin nickel. Over-all height, 22 inches; top diameter, 14 inches. Price, $10.00 each.

CHROMIUM AND COPPER FINISHES

Chase products come to you properly finished for their use. We are adding a few words of explanation here of these finishes and their care.

Copper Finish

Many Chase products are finished in polished or satin copper. In all cases the word "Copper" is used to designate the finish of the article, and not necessarily the basic metal underneath. While the basic metal used is always a non-rustable copper, or copper alloy, we have in many cases slightly alloyed the copper at an extra expense in order to give additional strength and hardness. Pure copper, although cheaper, is apt to be a little soft for such uses as beer mugs and bowls, and the addition of another metal greatly increases the tensile strength and hardness of the finished product, making it less liable to dent or bend even with hard usage.

Chase Chromium

Chromium is not a basic metal as many people suppose, but an extremely hard and durable finish that is plated over a brass or copper base that has first been nickel plated.

It should require no polishing, and no abrasive powders or cleaning liquids should be used. If the product is washed in soap and water and rubbed briskly with a dry cloth, the chromium finish should retain a permanent lustre and brilliance.

WHOLESALE PRICE LIST

Pages 6 and 7

ELECTRIC BUFFET SERVER   No. 27011
Each $20.00

Page 8

VIKING SAUCE BOWL   No. 17046
Each $1.75

LOTUS SAUCE BOWL   No. 17045
Each $1.75

CHEESE SERVER, Complete   No. 09009
Each $5.00

CHEESE SERVER, Tray only   No. 09010
Each $3.00

Page 9

SALAD BOWL   No. 27006
Each $3.00

JAM SET   No. 90018
Per Dozen $14.40

BREAKFAST SET, Complete   No. 26003
Each $1.50

BREAKFAST SET, Without Tray   No. 26001
Each $1.25

Page 10

HOT SERVICE COVER (Small)   No. 90006
Each $1.50

HOT SERVICE COVER (Large)   No. 90007
Each $1.75

COASTER SET   No. 11261
Per Dozen Sets of Four $7.20
Per Box of One Dozen $1.50

TRIPLE TRAY   No. 09001
Each $3.00

Page 11

TRAY   No. NS - 287
COPPER, Each $1.50
CHROMIUM, Each $2.00

INDIVIDUAL CANAPE PLATE   No. 27001
Per Dozen $7.20

TIFFIN TRAY   No. 17027
Each $3.75

Page 12

SERVING TRAY   No. 09002
COPPER, Each $3.00
CHROMIUM, Each $3.50

ROUND TRAY   No. 09011
COPPER, Per Dozen $3.60
CHROMIUM, Per Dozen $4.50

INFORMAL SERVING TRAY   No. 09012
Per Dozen $14.40

Page 13

SANDWICH PLATE   No. 27003
Each $2.00

COLD MEAT PLATTER   No. 27004
Each $2.00

BREAD TRAY   No. 27005
Each $1.75

SERVICE PLATE   No. 27002
Per Dozen $18.00

Pages 14 and 15

ARCHITEX CENTERPIECE, Complete   No. 27012
Per Set $10.00

ARCHITEX CENTERPIECE, Circular   No. 27008
Per Dozen $12.00

ARCHITEX CENTERPIECE, Rectangular   No. 27009
Per Dozen $12.00

ARCHITEX CANDLESTICK   No. 27007
Per Dozen $12.00

Page 16

TAUREX CANDLESTICK   No. 24004 & No. 24003
Each $1.50

SUNDAY SUPPER CANDLE HOLDERS   No. 24002
Per Dozen Sets of Four $7.20

DISC CANDLESTICKS   No. 24005
Each $2.00

Page 17

DIPLOMAT COFFEE SET, With Tray
Each $10.00

DIPLOMAT COFFEE SET Only   No. 17029
Each $7.50

DIPLOMAT TRAY Only   No. 17030
Each $2.50

TABLE BELLS   Nos. 13002, 13003, 13004, 13005
Per Dozen $7.20

Page 18

COCKTAIL TRAY   No. 09013
Per Dozen $14.40

COCKTAIL SHAKER   No. 90034
Each $2.00

COCKTAIL CUP   No. 26002
Per Dozen $3.60

Page 19

NIBLICK SWIZZLERS   No. 90037
Per Dozen Sets $3.60

CANDY DISH   No. 90011
Per Dozen $7.50

CONFECTION BOWL   No. 90027
Per Dozen $5.40

Page 20

IMPERIAL BOWL   No. 15003
Each $3.00

TROPHY VASE   No. 03005
Each $2.00

CALYX VASE (Small)   No. 03007
COPPER, Per Dozen $7.20
CHROMIUM, Per Dozen $9.00

CALYX VASE (Large)   No. 03008
COPPER, Per Dozen $10.80
CHROMIUM, Per Dozen $13.20

Page 21

FOUR TUBE BUD HOLDER   No. 11230
COMB. BRASS AND COPPER OR
CHROMIUM, Each $7.20

VICTORIAN VASE   No. 03006
Per Dozen $9.00

RING VASE   No. 17039
GOLDEN TRIANGLE METAL, Per Dozen . . .$15.00
CHROMIUM, Per Dozen $18.00

Page 23

BACCHUS GOBLET   No. 90032
Per Dozen $9.00

BEER MUG   No. 90042
COPPER, Per Gross $31.68
CHROMIUM, Per Dozen $3.60

CHESHIRE MUG   No. 90031
Per Dozen $7.20

Page 24

PRETZEL BOWL   No. 15004
Per Dozen $12.00

BACCHUS PITCHER   No. 90036
COPPER, Each $2.50
CHROMIUM, Each $3.00

PRETZELMAN   No. 90038
COPPER, Per Dozen $7.20
CHROMIUM, Per Dozen $10.80

Page 25

SALEM WATER PITCHER   No. 90004
Each $2.50

DEVONSHIRE PITCHER   No. 90025
COPPER, Each $1.50
CHROMIUM, Each $1.75

TAVERN PITCHER   No. 17026
Each $3.00

Page 26

FRENCH WATERING CAN   No. 05001
Each $5.00

RAIN-BEAU WATERING CAN   No. 05002
COMB. BRASS AND COPPER, Per Dozen . . . $7.20

Page 27

PENDANT PLANT BOWL   No. 04004
Per Dozen $7.20

ROUND ROD WALL BRACKET   No. 90029
Per Dozen $3.60

MAGNO GARDEN MARKER   No. 11108
Per Dozen $1.08

Page 28

INDOOR FLOWER CULTIVATOR   No. 11233
Per Dozen $1.75

RIBBED FLOWER POT   No. 04003
Per Dozen $7.20

FLOWER POT HOLDER   No. 11155
Per Dozen $7.20

Page 29

CAT DOOR STOP   No. 90035
Per Dozen $9.00

FOOTSCRAPER   No. 90033
Per Dozen $9.00

WEATHER VANE   No. 90030
Per Dozen $7.20

Page 30

GLOW LAMP   No. 01001
COPPER OR COMB. BLACK AND
CHROMIUM, Per Dozen $7.50
CHROMIUM, Each $9.60

FLUTED BASE TABLE LAMP   No. 01005
Each $3.75

DESK LAMP   No. 01003
Each $3.00

Page 31

CONSTELLATION LAMP No. 17048
Per Dozen $14.40
CIRCLE LAMP No. 01004
Each $2.50
SHIP AHOY LIGHT No. 01006
Per Dozen $14.40

Page 32

REEDED LAMP No. 01009
Per Dozen $10.80
CENTURY LAMP No. 01008
Each $3.00
TANKARD LAMP No. 01007
Per Dozen $7.80

Page 33

BALL LAMP No. 11235
Each $3.75
CONSOLE LAMP No. 27010
Each $3.75

Page 34

"BOMB" FLASHLIGHT No. 22001
Per Dozen $7.20
"AIRALITE" No. 22003
Per Dozen $5.40

Page 35

COLONEL LIGHT No. 27013
Per Dozen $12.00
BINNACLE LIGHTS No. 25001-2
Per Dozen $7.20

Page 36

VANITY MIRROR No. 90043
Per Dozen $1.80
HANDY DRYER No. 11232
Per Gross $21.00
SEWPACT No. 90026
Per Dozen $7.20

Page 37

THE VANITY ARISTOCRAT No. 1002A
Per Gross $54.00
DUPLEX PINPACK No. 1001
Per Gross $9.00
DUPLEX PINPACK DISPLAY CABINET No. 1001A
Each $2.25

Page 38

MIRROR TOP BOX No. 21003
Per Dozen $9.00
OCCASIONAL BOX No. 90002
Per Dozen $7.20

Page 39

THE ROLLAROUND No. 841
Per Dozen $14.40
CONNOISSEUR No. 842
Per Dozen $7.80

Page 40

ROUNDABOUT ASH TRAY No. 821
Per Dozen $1.80
ARISTOCRAT ASH TRAY No. 835
Per Dozen $7.20
TIP TILT ASH TRAY No. 819
Per Dozen $1.80
THE "FOURSOME" ASH RECEIVER SET No. 844
Per Dozen Sets $7.20

Page 41

SMOKESTACK No. 831
Per Dozen $7.20
CIGARETTE SERVER & ASH TRAY No. 824
Per Dozen $3.75
HUMPTY DUMPTY ASH TRAY No. 500
Per Dozen $3.60

Page 42

HI-LO SMOKERS' STAND No. 836
Per Dozen $10.80
ECLIPSE ASH TRAY No. 809
Per Dozen $5.40

Page 43

NOB-TOP ASH TRAY No. 810
Per Dozen $5.40
PENTAD ASH RECEIVERS No. 840
Per Dozen Sets $6.00
FLUTED ASH TRAYS No. 17040
Per Dozen Sets of Four $7.20

Page 44

SWAN ASH TRAY No. 837
Per Dozen $6.00
COMPACT CIGARETTTE SERVER No. 822
Per Dozen $7.20
AUTOMATIC TABLE LIGHTER No. 825
Per Dozen $7.20

Page 45

FOUR PIECE SMOKERS' SET No. 823
Per Dozen $7.20
MATCH PACK ASH TRAY No. 820
Per Dozen $7.20
CROWN ASH TRAY No. 811
Each $0.90

Page 46

CIGARETTE SERVER AND ASH TRAY No. 806
Each $0.90
AUTOMATIC LIGHTER AND TRAY No. 828
Per Dozen $12.00
DE LUXE CIGARETTE SET No. 815
Each $3.00

Page 47

"LAZY BOY" SMOKERS' STAND No. 17031
Each $6.00

CHASE

CHROMIUM
BRASS & COPPER
SPECIALTIES

CHASE CHROMIUM BRASS & COPPER SPECIALTIES

CHROMIUM IS BEST OVER BRASS OR COPPER

CHASE CHROMIUM BRASS & COPPER SPECIALTIES

CHROMIUM IS BEST OVER BRASS OR COPPER

CHASE CHROMIUM BRASS & COPPER SPECIALTIES

CHROMIUM IS BES BRASS OR COPPER

CHASE

CHASE CHROMIUM BRASS & COPPER SPECIALTIES

CHROMIUM IS BEST OVER BRASS OR COPPER

CHASE CHROMIUM BRASS & COPPER SPECIALTIES

CHROMIUM IS BEST OVER BRASS OR COPPER

CHASE CHROMIUM BRASS & COPPER SPECIALTIES

CHROMIUM IS BEST OVER BRASS OR COPPER

CHASE CHROMIUM BRASS & COPPER SPECIALTIES

Chase Tower Holds
New York's Finest
Specialty Display Rooms

We urge all our friends to come and visit us when they are in New York at our new show rooms in Chase Tower at 10 East 40th Street, New York City. The rooms are decorated by Ruth Gerth, and the deep blue ceilings and white venetian blinds make an unusual and fascinating background for Chase products.

Part of the space is given to a model shop, "Chase Specialty Shop." Here are shown various ways to display Chase copper, Chase bronze, and Chase chromium goods. There are shop windows with modern window displays, and inside the shop itself are buffet tables and counter displays.

Chromium

"Chromium," Mrs. Emily Post says, "is the answer to the house-wife's prayer, appealing not only to the eye, but to practical requirements, for it stays brilliantly polished to the end of time."

Should Be Plated Over Brass

But chromium is only as good as the metal it is plated on. If chromium is plated over a rustable metal, sooner or later rust is liable to form underneath the chromium plate which will begin to chip and peel.

Fine Old English Sheffield silver was always plated over copper. And so Chase chromium is plated over solid non-rusting brass or copper. The chromium and the brass make a solid bond and preserve this hard brilliant plating indefinitely.

Remember when buying chromium to ask whether it is plated over brass or over a rustable metal. The answer will tell you the life and value of the article.

Chromium for the House-Wife

While many Chase products are also made in brass and copper, most of them are made in chromium. For chromium is the modern metal. It harmonizes with modern furnishings, and reflects the brilliance and spirit of our age.

But chromium owes a great share of its popularity to the house-wife, who has found to her delight that it doesn't tarnish and never has to be polished. Chromium is becoming more and more popular as people understand its great advantage. But be sure that it is Chase chromium over copper or brass.

New Chase Specialties for 1935

This year Chase has produced many interesting novelties for the department stores and gift shops. They are not only perfect gift and bridge prizes, but they have a year 'round appeal because of their durability and everlasting brilliance.

Notice as you go through the catalog such novel products as the Continental Coffee Making Service, the Chase Mechanical Candles, the Cocktail Canapé Server, the Rockwell Kent Cigarette Box, the Snack Server, and many others. You will find designs by the foremost American artists. You will see novelty and cleverness. But best of all notice that each item is designed for its use.

Design and Value

We thank our friends for their support of us and their enthusiasm in promoting our products. Their wide acceptance by the public shows we have made no mistake in the selection of our designers, and in the type and quality of merchandise that we are producing.

Other products that imitate the fine work of these artists will probably appear. Chromium instead of being plated over non-rusting brass will be put over inferior metals, giving the articles short life.

We expect such cheapening of merchandise, but we will continue to refuse to lower the quality of design and finish that have made Chase Chromium, Brass and Copper Specialties, nationally known and asked for by name.

Nationally Advertised

This year you will find more and more people who will come to you asking for our products by name. They will come to you because of our national advertising and constant promotion of these products, and they will also come because they appreciate fine things, and recognize that the well-known Chase trade-mark stands for a mark of quality in metal specialties.

TERMS

The prices shown in this catalog are retail prices. Discounts from retail prices are listed numerically according to article number on a separate confidential Price List and Dealers' Discount Sheet. Prices and discounts are subject to change without notice.

The minimum order accepted by us is $10.00 for accounts now on our books, and $50.00 from new accounts.

2% discount will be allowed on all invoices paid on or before the tenth of month following date of shipment, F.O.B. factory, Waterbury, Conn.

If a sales tax is enacted, it will be added to the invoice covering the shipment of any article referred to in this catalog.

CHASE BRASS & COPPER CO.
—INCORPORATED—
SUBSIDIARY OF KENNECOTT COPPER CORPORATION

SPECIALTY SALES DIVISION • CHASE TOWER • 10 EAST 40TH STREET, NEW YORK CITY

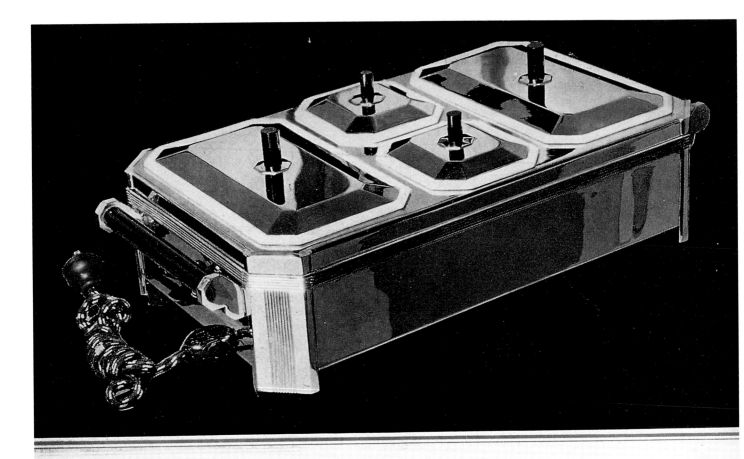

Chase Electric Buffet Server

No. 27011

The Chase Electric Buffet Server, designed for Chase by Lurelle Guild, is an electrically heated dish that makes it possible to keep **four kinds of food** hot on the buffet table without overcooking. Late guests do not worry the hostess because food stays hot and attractive for hours if necessary. For hot buffet suppers and lunches, for late Sunday breakfasts, and late evening entertaining, the server is invaluable. Up to twenty people can be served from it. In the Summer the server can be filled with cracked ice for cold foods such as salads, cold soups and desserts, etc.

Mrs. Emily Post says about the Chase Buffet Server: "There is now a very last word in buffet equipment . . . a buffet server. It is quite the most delectable novelty that has been produced; to me at least, it is completely tempting. Its design is modernistic, as is suitable in the polished chromium of which it is made, and yet its simplicity of design that relies for its ornamentation on octagonal outline and ivory edging and ebony handles, would be entirely in key with almost any type of house. It holds four deep casserole dishes, two large and two small, set into a smart tray-shaped box filled with water kept by an electric element at an exact temperature."

DESCRIPTION

The Chase Electric Buffet Server is a giant hot water dish, in chromium, half filled with water which is kept between 160° and 180° by a concealed electric heating element. Into the receptacle with its electrically heated water are placed four porcelain casserole dishes, two large (2½ quart capacity) and two small (1½ pint capacity). Foods can be cooked right in these dishes which have chromium covers with black composition handles. The server has two long composition bar handles so that it can be moved easily. It operates on either A.C. or D.C. current, 110 to 120 volt circuit, 25, 40 or 60 cycles, and has a current consumption of 1/7 kilowatt per hour. Over-all, the server is 18 inches long, 11 inches wide and 5 inches high. If 220 volts is desired order No. 27029.

MECHANICAL OPERATION

To fill the server, the casseroles are removed and the server is filled with boiling water up to the water line clearly marked along the side of the interior. The electric plug is then attached to the regular house electric circuit in any convenient receptacle outlet. The casserole dishes are filled with their proper foods in the kitchen, and brought in and placed in the electric buffet server in the dining room. The covers are put on, and the food is ready to serve at once, or hours later. Because the electric heat will never heat the water too much, the food in the casseroles cannot burn and will not cook as in the ordinary chafing dish, or hot plate. The Chase Electric Buffet Server has been tested and approved by Good Housekeeping Institute. Price, $45.00 each.

A book "How to Give Buffet Suppers" by Emily Post is furnished free with each buffet server. Additional copies can be obtained for 10 cents in stamps, or 5 cents each in quantities for trade use.

CHASE

CHASE CHROMIUM BRASS & COPPER SPECIALTIES

Chase Electric Snack Server

No. 90048

The Electric Snack Server is an electrically heated dish with three food compartments, or casseroles. Food can be prepared in advance and be served two or three, or more, hours later without bother or delay. It is designed for serving warm luncheons for small families or parties where four to eight people are to be served. The golf foursome, for instance, can return home after a late game and find a hot supper waiting for them. Bridge parties can continue at cards without the usual interruption for the preparation of "something to eat."

The new Chase Snack Server is not intended, and should not be sold, as a substitute for the Chase Electric Buffet Server. Although both the Buffet Server and the Snack Server keep food hot and appetizing, their use varies greatly. Whereas the Buffet Server has a large capacity (6½ quarts) and is used for serving large groups, the Snack Server has a total capacity of only three quarts, which, of course, limits its use to the serving of small families and parties.

The design of the Snack Server is outstanding. It is circular in shape and has three one-quart food containers fitted with smart looking "stepped-down" covers. The server is of gleaming chromium, while the fittings are of wood finished with a lustrous black surface. The casseroles are Pyrex glass, which will

stand extremely high temperatures. Food can be cooked right in these containers and then put in the Snack Server to be kept hot.

The operation of the Snack Server is similar to that of the Buffet Server. With the casseroles removed, the server is filled with boiling water up to the water line marked on the inside. The electric plug is attached to any convenient receptacle outlet and the current turned on. The casseroles are brought in from the kitchen filled with the food to be served and placed in the server. The covers are put on and the preparation of a luncheon to be served immediately, or sometime later, is completed. There is no possibility of overcooking or burning—the temperature is maintained between 160° and 180°, a proper serving temperature but too low for cooking. The server operates on standard 110 to 120 volt current, either alternating or direct, 25, 40 or 60 cycles and consumes one-seventh of a kilowatt per hour. This consumption rate, based on an average cost of six cents per kilowatt, means that the Snack Server can be operated at less than one cent per hour!

On hot Summer days and evenings when cold salads are more appetizing than hot luncheons, fill the server with cracked ice, which will chill the food and keep it cold until it is served.

CHASE

The Electric Snack Server is 13 inches in diameter, and 6 inches high. It is available in one finish only, chromium, with black fittings. Price, $19.50 each.

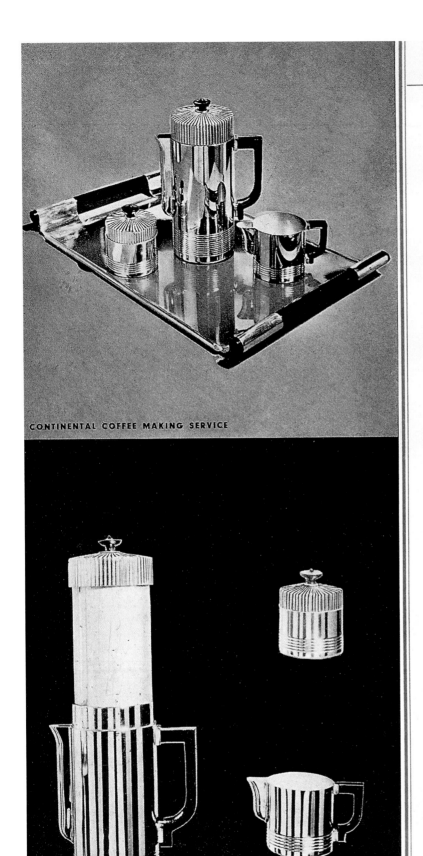

CONTINENTAL COFFEE MAKING SERVICE

COFFEE POT ASSEMBLED FOR MAKING COFFEE

Continental Coffee-Making Service

No. 17054

Here, at last, is something new in coffee sets. Most experts agree on two cardinal rules of making coffee:

1. The "Drip" method, used in France and other European countries, makes the clearest freshest coffee.

2. Coffee should be made and served in the same pot. By serving it from the pot it was brewed in, all the richness of its flavor is retained.

We are all familiar with the old-fashioned glass balls heated over flame so common abroad. They are efficient but they lack good looks. Other "drip type" utensils look like the kitchen and usually stay there.

The new Chase Continental Coffee-Making Service has three great advantages:

1. It makes coffee by the drip method.

2. Coffee is served from the pot it was made in.

3. It is made of non-tarnishing chromium, and beautifully designed by Walter Von Nessen for Chase in a beautiful new modern design.

DESCRIPTION

The three-piece set, consisting of sugar bowl, cream pitcher and combination coffee-making-and-serving pot, is finished in gleaming polished chromium. The handles and knobs are of polished jet black composition. A series of narrow ribs or rings encircle the lower part of the straight-walled cylindrical pieces. Above these rings is an unbroken mirror-like expanse which reflects surrounding objects, lights and colors. The tops of the sugar bowl and coffee pot are decorated with vertical ribs which converge in the center of the top. The long spouts provide easy pouring without dripping.

CONSTRUCTION

As its name implies, the Continental Coffee-Making Service is actually a coffee making set, complete and compact. The coffee pot is fitted with an inner shell which is set on top of the pot when making coffee. This shell, or water basket, has several tiny holes in its bottom to permit water to seep very slowly into the small coffee container fitted on the bottom of the basket. Six cups can be made at one time.

INSTRUCTIONS

Complete detailed instructions for making coffee are included with each Continental Coffee Pot.

DIMENSIONS AND PRICE

The Continental Coffee Pot only, 9⅜ inches high and 3¾ inches in diameter, No. 17051, retails at $10.00. Sugar Bowl only, 3⅝ inches high and 3 inches in diameter, No. 17052, $4.00. Cream Pitcher only, 2⅞ inches high and 3 inches in diameter, No. 17053, $6.00. Three-piece set complete, $20.00 each. Set with No. 17027 Tiffin Tray, as illustrated, $29.00.

CHASE

Chase Mechanical Candles
and
Fire-Resisting Shades

Nos. 24006—24007   Nos. 90049—90050

Long dresses, veils, even bustles and Mid-Victorian furniture are staging a come-back. And Chase now presents, for 1935, the romantically shaded candlelight of our mothers' and grandmothers' day.

For too many years have we had dinner tables with the glaring blinding light of stark and unshielded candles. Now we can have soft flattering shielded light, shaded from our eyes and yet directed down on the flowers, chromium, glass and china table pieces.

Until now there has been no way of fastening candle-shades to the candles which rapidly shortened as they burned. Chase Mechanical Candle always stays at the same height. It never burns lower, and yet the candle burns down to its last half inch! (Such economy!).

The Chase Mechanical Candle is a hollow metal tube, looking exactly like a candle, inside of which a real candle is placed. A spring forces the candle up to the top of the tube, and as it burns, the spring forces the candle up through the tube, keeping it always at the same height automatically. After a few moments of burning a small cup forms at the top which prevents dripping and allows the candle to burn to the extreme end. The candle lasts longer because the wax is not melted and dripped away but is completely consumed in giving light.

The tube is finished to resemble a pure white candle and the chromium spring holder at the bottom is tapered to fit nearly all candlesticks. Comes complete with satin chromium shade holder. Packed six to a carton with counter display to aid selling. Furnished in two sizes: No. 24006, 10½ inches long; No. 24007, 7 inches long. Price, $1.00 each. "Talisman," a fire-resisting pleated silk shade, rose color, No. 90050, $1.00 each. "Victory," a translucent shade in powder blue with chromium wreath decoration and silver edging, fire-resisting, No. 90049, $1.00 each.

Athena Candelabra
No. 27030

We are particularly fond of the lovely symmetry of line, beautifully carried out in this new Athena Candelabra. Its fluted vertical column and highly polished chromium finish make it one of the smartest of modern designs. Candle holders are on either side of a central "stepped-up" glass finial. The simple circular base is heavily weighted to avoid tipping. It stands 13½ inches high and looks particularly attractive with candles of medium height. We recommend Chase Mechanical Candles with the "Victory" shades. The base is 5 inches in diameter. Price, packed in gift box, $15.00 each.

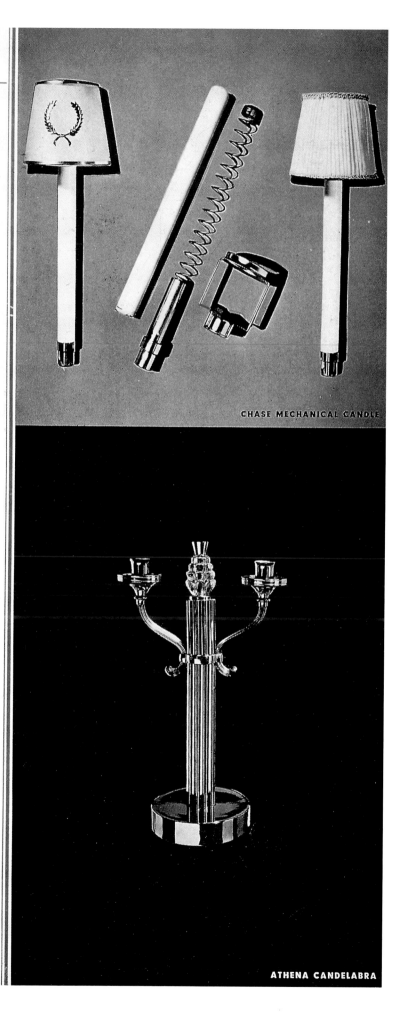

CHASE MECHANICAL CANDLE

ATHENA CANDELABRA

ARCHITEX ADJUSTABLE CENTERPIECE

Architex Adjustable Centerpiece
No. 27012

This decorative centerpiece consists of ten pieces; four square candlesticks, four quarter-circle flower boxes, and two rectangular flower boxes. These pieces can be grouped to form many designs. The centerpiece* can be large and spread out or small and friendly, modernistic or conventional. One of the rectangular boxes with candle-boxes at either end make a charming centerpiece for a small table. A wire flower holder is furnished with each box. Polished chromium finish with black legs. Price complete, $20.00. Individual pieces, No. 27007 candlestick; No. 28008 circular centerpiece; No. 28009 rectangular centerpiece; $2.00 each.

*Send for free folder of suggestions on grouping arrangements and use of flowers and candles.

FIESTA FLOWER BOWL

Fiesta Flower Bowl
No. 29002

This graceful bowl, designed by the Gerths, gets its name from the Spanish word "fiesta", which means "a joyous and gay holiday or festivity when flowers play an important part in decoration." Here at last is a properly designed flower bowl. It is open enough at the top to spread out the flowers; small enough at the bottom to hold the stems from slipping; and it is deep enough to hold plenty of water and to support the stems properly. The reflections of the colored flowers and surrounding objects in the highly polished outside surface give a charming effect. From an 8-inch top diameter the bowl tapers in gradually until with a well rounded curve it reaches the 4-inch wooden base. Overall it is 6 inches high. Available in polished chromium with black base, or polished copper with walnut base. Price, $6.00.

FIESTA CANDLESTICKS

Fiesta Candlesticks
No. 29001

Although these unusual candlesticks were designed as companion pieces to the Fiesta Flower Bowl, they do not depend on the bowl for their smartness. The Fiesta Candlesticks mounted on a wooden base resemble an upright hoop, the ends of which form the candle holders. The small wooden collars underneath the candle holders are in keeping with the base. Finished in polished chromium with black wood base and collars, or polished copper, with walnut base and collars. Designed by the Gerths. Size: 8 inches wide, 8⅜ inches high, 3⅞ inch base diameter. Price, $6.00.

CHASE

Taurex Candlesticks

No. 24003   No. 24004

A reasonably priced candlestick designed to hold two candles in the new smart even and uneven arrangement. For a suggestion, display them in chromium with one blue and one green candle; or, in copper with one green and one brown candle. Finished in polished chromium, satin copper or polished copper. Packed one in a gift box. The uneven candle holder, No. 24004, is 9¾ inches high. The even candle holder, No. 24003, is 7⅛ inches high. Price, $3.00 each.

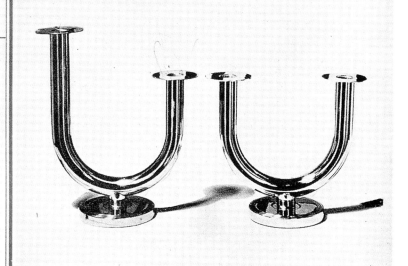

TAUREX CANDLESTICKS

Imperial Bowl

No. 15003

This graceful fruit or flower bowl is made of satin copper with a satin silver lining and black nickel base, or polished chromium with satin silver lining and black nickel base. The piece stands 4 inches high and is 8½ inches in diameter. Packed in attractive gift box. Price, either finish, $7.50 each.

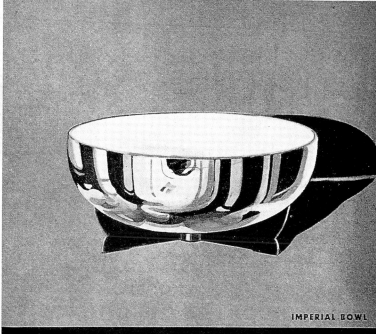

IMPERIAL BOWL

Disc Candlestick

No. 24005

This smart candlestick, designed by the Gerths, combining discs with a sphere, holds two candles. The flat polished surfaces reflect the lights and colors of the dinner table. This candlestick is exceptionally good looking with tall dark navy-blue candles. Height 4¾ inches, width 8½ inches. Finished in polished chromium or satin copper. Price, $4.50 each.

DISC CANDLESTICK

CHASE

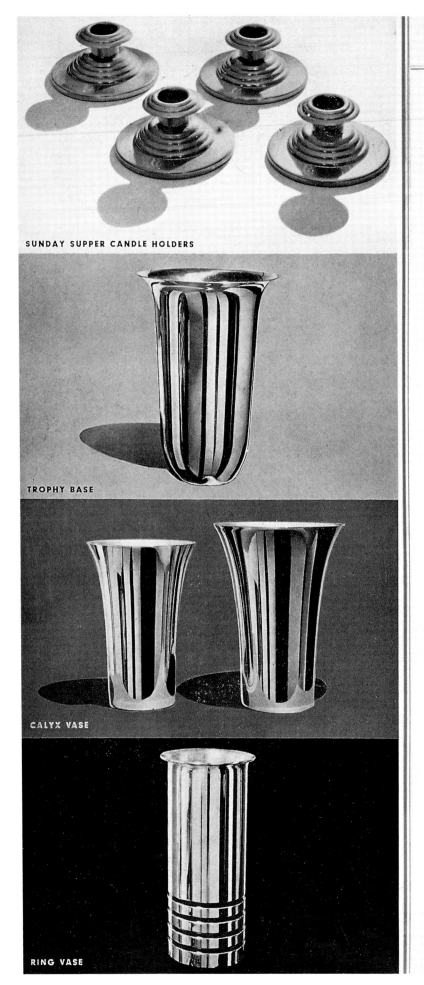

SUNDAY SUPPER CANDLE HOLDERS

TROPHY BASE

CALYX VASE

RING VASE

Sunday Supper Candle Holders

No. 24002

Designed to fit into any scheme of decoration and excellent to use in groups on the dining table. They are low and easy to look over. They are well balanced and look exceptionally well with tall candles. Try using eight of them, alternating high and low colored candles, in a circle around the Imperial Bowl. Height 1¾ inches, diameter 3⅜ inches. Finished in black nickel, polished copper, satin brass, or satin nickel. A set of four in attractive gift box. Price, $1.00 per set .

Trophy Vase

No. 03005

Tall and tapered toward the base similar to the traditional loving cup. The graceful flared top will accommodate large bouquets. If possible display them with artificial flowers. Diameter of base 3 inches; height 9 inches. In three finishes: triangle metal (golden) satin finish, chromium, and black nickel. Price, $4.00 each.

Calyx Vase

No. 03007-8

This smartly flared vase has a simplicity of design that is refreshing. Either the polished copper or the polished chromium assures a graceful container for cut flowers. It is available in two convenient sizes. The small size (No. 03007) is 6½ inches high. Price: either polished copper or chromium, $1.50 each. The large size (No. 03008) is 7½ inches high. Price: either polished copper or chromium, $2.00 each.

Ring Vase

No. 17039

Four rings of colorful enamel and a rolled top stress the simplicity and beauty of this vase for tall flowers. A pair for a mantle-piece balances perfectly. Height 9½ inches. Diameter 4 inches. Finished in chromium with black rings, or golden triangle metal with rings of lapis blue. One to a gift box. Price, $2.25 each.

Fruit Bowl

No. 17007

Walter Von Nessen designed this graceful bowl that will hold an ample quantity of fruit, nuts or candy. From the 9½ inch top diameter the sides slope gradually to a 3¼ inch base. 3 inches high. The top edge is beaded. Finished in polished chromium or polished copper. Price, $6.00 each.

Ribbed Flower Pot

No. 04003

A large enough flower pot with a very different and attractive design. The close ribbed treatment is modern in feeling and yet harmonizes with old furnishings. And the graceful spread at the top catches any excess water when watering. Height 5⅜ inches. Finished in satin copper. One to a gift box. Price, $1.00 each.

Flower Pot Holder

No. 11155

In a modern stepped-down design, with saucer to match. May be had in polished brass or polished copper. Diameter 5¾ inches, height 4½ inches. Individually packed in attractive gift box. Price, $1.00 each.

Indoor Flower Cultivator

No. 11233

A combination rake and spade for loosening the earth in potted plants. Finished in combination polished brass and copper. Individually boxed. Price, 25c. each.

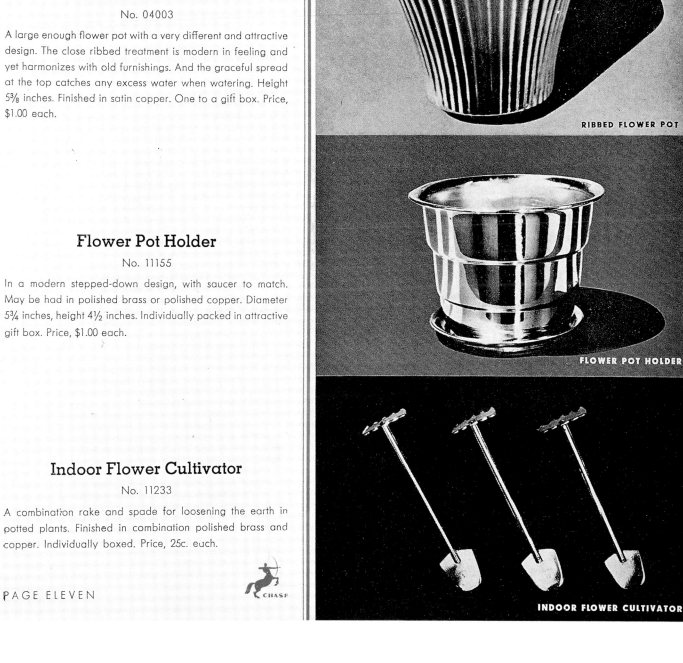

FRUIT BOWL

RIBBED FLOWER POT

FLOWER POT HOLDER

INDOOR FLOWER CULTIVATOR

VIKING SAUCE BOWL

LOTUS SAUCE BOWL

JAM SET

DIPLOMAT COFFEE SET WITH TRAY

Viking Sauce Bowl

No. 17046

This is one of the most beautifully designed bowls we have ever made. It was designed for mayonnaise, French dressing, gravy or fruit sauces. It is ideal for a wedding gift, attractively finished in polished chromium outside and satin chromium inside. The bowl handle is of black composition. Complete with ladle and tray to match. Price, $4.00 each.

Lotus Sauce Bowl

No. 17045

Like an open lotus blossom the lovely design of this bowl is a delight to look at. For mayonnaise, gravy, or fruit sauces it is perfect. Finished in polished chromium outside and satin chromium inside. Black composition handle. Complete with ladle and tray to match. Price, $4.00 each.

Jam Set

No. 90018

With metal cover and tray finished in satin copper, the hobnail glass jar is in a blush pink tone with a glass spoon to match. It is also made with chromium lid and tray with clear glass jar and spoon. Height 5¼ inches. Diameter 6⅜ inches. Packed in gift box. Price, $2.50 each.

Diplomat Coffee Set with Tray

Coffee Set No. 17029 Tray No. 17030

This beautiful Chase coffee set designed by Walter Von Nessen is now used in many famous American homes. It has appeared in well-known Broadway plays, and in some of the most popular moving pictures. Well-known theatrical stars and society leaders have chosen it for their drawing rooms. The Diplomat set is modern in design and yet it blends perfectly with more conservative home furnishings. We recommend the set highly as typifying the best and most sincere in modern American design.

The coffee pot, sugar bowl and creamer come in polished chromium, or polished copper with white tinned lining inside. The handles and knobs are of highly polished black composition. Dimensions: coffee pot, diameter 2⅜ inches, height over-all 8 inches; sugar bowl, diameter 2⅜ inches, height over-all 4 inches; creamer, diameter 2⅜ inches, height 2¾ inches. The black mirror-like tray is available with the rolled edge in chromium or polished copper. Diameter of tray 10 inches. Coffee Set, price, $17.50. Tray, price, $6.00.

CHASE

Triple Tray

No. 09001

This will hold a variety of cakes or sandwiches and takes little space on the table. It is collapsible and can easily be put away in a drawer when not in use. This lovely tray is chromium plated over non-rusting brass. Size (folded up) 7½ inches by 11 inches. Finished in polished chromium. Packed in attractive gift box. Price, $6.00 each.

Round Tray

No. 17006

A sturdy tray of beautiful design to hold many glasses. It is 12 inches in diameter and has a small beaded flange about ¾ inch high. Available in polished copper, satin copper, or polished chromium. Individually packed. Price, $5.00 each.

Salver

No. 90010

This large tray for fruit presents an appearance of magnificence when centered on a dining table or sideboard in a large room covered with grape or ivy leaves, apples, oranges, bananas and grapes,—it makes a centerpiece never to be forgotten. It measures 20 inches in diameter and has three evenly spaced steps to the center. Finished in satin copper. Price, $10.00.

Tiffin Tray

No. 17027

An unusual strongly built serving tray that holds a lot without crowding. It will hold the Diplomat Coffee Set and four demi-tasse cups easily, and goes well with the new Continental Coffee Making Service. It was designed by Walter Von Nessen. Length 18 inches, width 12 inches. In beautiful polished chromium, satin copper or polished copper with black handles. Price, $9.00 each.

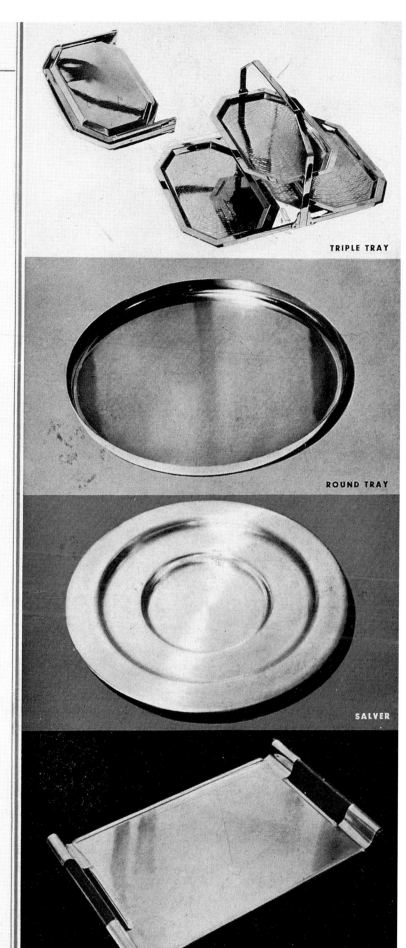

TRIPLE TRAY

ROUND TRAY

SALVER

TIFFIN TRAY

BREAKFAST SET

PANCAKE AND CORN SET

SALT AND PEPPER SPHERES

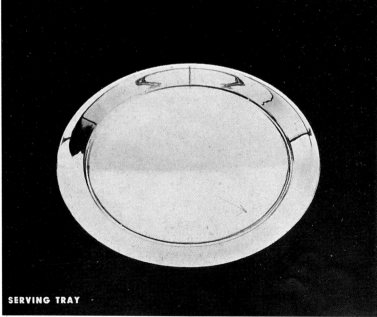

SERVING TRAY

Breakfast Set

No. 26003 complete   No. 26001 without tray

The Gerths designed this three-piece set of semi-spherical design, one of the most popular of Chase Specialties. The brilliance of the highly polished sugar bowl and creamer is set off by the black handles. An etched design decorates the tray. Dimensions: sugar bowl 4¼ inches high, 3¾ inches in diameter; creamer 3⅛ inches in diameter, 4⅞ inches long over-all; tray 11⅜ inches long, 5 inches wide, ⅜ inch in depth. Finished in polished chromium. Prices: set complete $3.00 each; without tray, $2.50 each.

Pancake and Corn Set

No. 28003

This amusing four-piece set designed by Russell Wright in polished chromium will add sparkle and color to any table setting. Deep blue glass forms the bottom of the tray. The pitcher may be used for syrup, drawn butter, cream, French dressing, or chocolate sauce for ice cream. The spheres will hold salt and pepper, powdered sugar and other condiments. Dimensions: pitcher 5¼ inches high; tray 6 inches in diameter; large sphere 1¾ inches in diameter; small sphere 1⅛ inches in diameter. Price, complete, $4.50; pitcher only (No. 28005), $2.00.

Salt and Pepper Spheres

No. 28004

These spherical shakers are the same as those in the Pancake and Corn Set described above. Finished in polished chromium. Price, per pair packed in gift box, $1.00.

Serving Tray

No. 09002

Here is a grand big tray for sandwiches or hors d'oeuvres, or salads. It is a huge help in serving refreshments or buffet meals. Diameter of tray is 18 inches. Finished in lustrous satin copper, polished copper, or polished chromium. Individually boxed. Price, $7.00 each. No. 09003, Fruit Tray (not illustrated) has wider flange. Price, $7.00 each.

CHASE

Wine Cooler

No. 27015

All white wines, sauterne and champagne, imported or domestic, should be iced before using, and kept in ice during use. Here is a wine cooler which never has to be polished and is, therefore, always ready to be used. Rockwell Kent, famous American artist-author has designed a beautiful decorative plaque for it. The child Bacchus, homeward bound with wine grapes, symbolizes the spirit of wine. This is the first time Mr. Kent has ever designed for metal. The cooler can also be used as a lovely flower vase for large flowers or laurel. It is 9¼ inches high, and 8½ inches in diameter. Available in all-chromium finish, or combination polished brass and polished copper. Price, $12.00 each.

WINE COOLER

Wine Bottle Stand

No. 27016

The Wine Bottle Stand keeps dripping bottles from staining the table-cloth. It is particularly for red wine, but also for beer, ginger ale and other bottles. Plaque design is by Rockwell Kent. The stand is 4½ inches in diameter, and 2 inches high. Finished in polished chromium and combination polished brass and copper. Price, $1.25 each.

WINE BOTTLE STAND

Cocktail Canapé Server

No. 28001

The Cocktail Canapé Server is extremely useful for smart informal gatherings. The lower tray holds cocktails, while the upper tray holds hors d'oeuvres, canapés and appetizers. Small cocktail napkins tuck into the rings. We suggest alternate solid colored ones, such as red and white. The server requires but little space on the table and can be carried easily with food and drinks without danger of tipping or spilling. Overall height 13¾ inches; diameter of trays, top 12¾ inches, bottom 13¼ inches. May be disassembled for storage if desired. Polished chromium finish. Price, $12.50 each.

COCKTAIL CANAPÉ SERVER

CHASE

LIQUEUR SET

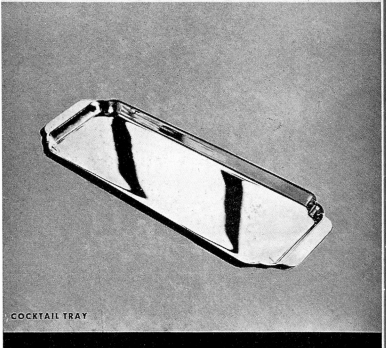

COCKTAIL TRAY

COCKTAIL SHAKER

Liqueur Set
No. 90046

This attractive set consists of six gleaming chromium Liqueur Cups (No. 90047) and a small round tray with deep English blue glass bottom. The small cups 2⅜ inches high, hold just enough and will not tip over easily. Furnished in polished chromium. Price, set complete, $4.00; Liqueur Cups only, 50c. each.

Coaster Tray
No. 09014

This tray is the same as that in the Liqueur Set described above. It is 6 inches in diameter and has a rolled edge in polished chromium about ¾ inch high. It can be used as a glass coaster, a card tray and for many other purposes. Price, $1.00 each.

Cocktail Tray
No. 09013

This simple cocktail tray is ideal for use with cocktail cups, No. 26002, (page 18), but may be used equally as well with other cocktail service pieces. It comes individually packed in either polished chromium, or polished copper finish. Over-all dimensions 15⅞ inches long, 5⅜ inches wide. Price, $2.50 each.

Cocktail Shaker
No. 90034

Entirely modern in its appearance, it retains the usefulness of old-fashioned shakers. The top is fitted with a sleeve which fits snugly into the pouring lip when shaking to prevent leaking or spilling of contents. A strainer is also provided to hold back the mint leaves, lemon rind, or other solids. Finished in bright chromium with choice of black, red or green enamel rings at top and bottom. Satin silver inside. Height 11½ inches; diameter 3¾ inches. Individually packed in gift box. Price, $4.50 each.

Ice Bowl and Tongs

No. 28002

This classic bowl, 7 inches in diameter designed for Chase by Russell Wright, holds an ample supply of ice in cracked or cube form. The bowl may also be used without the tongs for potato chips, pretzels, crackers, or nuts. The handle makes it easy to hold in passing food when entertaining. Finished in chromium or combination polished brass and polished copper. Price, complete with tongs, $4.50 each.

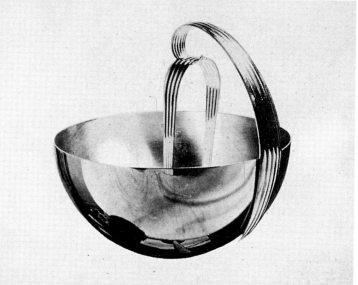

ICE BOWL AND TONGS

Cheese Server

No. 09009

There are certain good old rules for serving cheese. Cheese should be placed and cut on wood. It should be covered. And it should appear together with its crackers. This cheese server does all these things, and looks handsome besides. This server was designed for Chase by the Gerths. The tray is 14 inches in diameter and is built up from the center in three shallow steps on which crackers are arranged. Finished in lasting polished chromium. Prices: Cheese Server complete, $9.00; Tray only (No. 09010), $6.00 each.

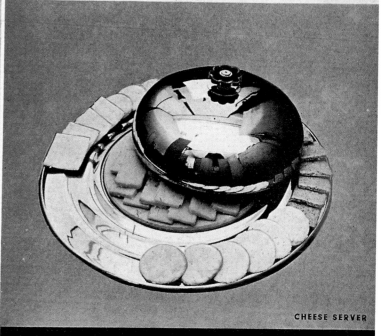

CHEESE SERVER

Stirring Cocktail Mixer

No. 17049

Some cocktails should be stirred—not shaken! This graceful mixer was designed for us by Walter Von Nessen. It holds one quart and has a guard which holds back the ice, but does not prevent perfect pouring. Beautifully finished in gleaming chromium outside, satin silver inside. Overall height 8¾ inches, base diameter 3 inches. Complete with long-handled stirring spoon designed to match the mixer, $5.00.

(Selected list of stirred cocktail recipes enclosed with each mixer).

STIRRING COCKTAIL MIXER

JIGGER AND SWIZZLER SET

COCKTAIL CUP

PRETZEL BOWL

PRETZELMAN

Jigger and Swizzler Set

No. 28017

This inexpensive chromium-finished set is a great help in mixing drinks. The amusing "High Hat" measuring jigger holds exactly a jiggerful (1½ oz.). The Niblick Swizzlers are thorough mixers when rotated between the palms of the hands or when used as puddlers. Set complete (Jigger and 4 Swizzlers) in gift box $1.00. "High-Hat" Jigger only, No. 28014, 1¾ inches high, 50c.; Niblick Swizzlers only, No. 90037, 7½ inches long, per set of four, 50c.

Cocktail Cup

No. 26002

Simplicity is an outstanding feature in the design of this distinctive cocktail cup, but it is the simplicity of line and decoration that suggests sophistication and good taste. The cup is 2 inches high, 2¾ inches in diameter and is finished in polished chromium outside and satin chromium inside. Price, 50c. each.

Pretzel Bowl

No. 15004

The charm of this pretzel bowl is in its restrained graceful simplicity. It is 7 inches in diameter at the top with a depth of 2⅝ inches and will hold quite a supply of pretzels, potato chips, nuts, crackers, candy, or cookies. The base is 3 inches in diameter. Finished in polished copper or polished chromium. Price, $3.00 each.

Pretzelman

No. 90038

This jolly, high-stepping, pretzelman holds a generous supply of pretzels above the beer glasses below. He was designed to be equally adept at carrying doughnuts or cookies with holes in them. He stands 18 inches high and is finished in gleaming copper or chromium. Prices: copper, $1.25 each; chromium, $2.00 each.

Cheshire Mug

No. 90031

Here's a tankard that smacks of Old England and its "Cheshire Cheese" tap room. Notice the unique semi-circular handle and the smooth rolled edge. A choice of finishes is offered; polished chromium, or polished copper with brass handle and white metal lining. 4 inches high, 3¼ inches diameter. Capacity 18 ounces. Price, $1.00 each.

Bacchus Goblet

No. 90032

A goblet which is suggestive of the Imperial wine feasts of Roman days. This design, coupled with its 18 ounce capacity makes the Bacchus Goblet a favorite. It's a grand glass to toast with! Height 6 inches, diameter 3 inches. Polished copper or chromium with white metal lining. Individually packed. Price, $1.25 each.

Bacchus Pitcher

No. 90036

Designed by the Gerths to use with Bacchus Goblets, this pitcher has the same attractive thumb-print design. The long, tapering pouring lip and the unusual shape of the handle add distinctiveness. Height 10¼ inches, width 8¾ inches, capacity three pints. Finshed in either polished copper or polished chromium. Price, $6.00 each.

Devonshire Pitcher

No. 90025

An old-but-new pitcher finished in either polished copper or chromium with a white metal lining. This roomy pitcher holds two quarts of ale or beer, milk, water or iced tea. In copper it is ideal for colonial settings, cellar tap rooms and terraces. In chromium it is modern enough for the newest furnishings. Packed one to a gift box. Price, $3.50 each.

CHESHIRE MUG

BACCHUS GOBLET

BACCHUS PITCHER

DEVONSHIRE PITCHER

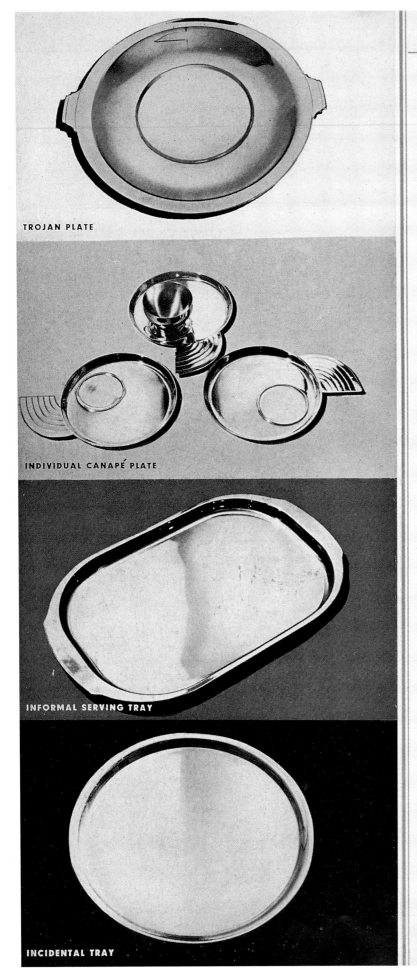

TROJAN PLATE

INDIVIDUAL CANAPÉ PLATE

INFORMAL SERVING TRAY

INCIDENTAL TRAY

Trojan Plate
No. 09004

Here is a practical sandwich plate finished in glistening chromium. The edge is grooved all the way around and the flat handles are an extension of the rim in modern stepped-down design. The flat surfaces of the handles are very suitable places for engraved monograms or initials. 12 inches in diameter. Price, $5.00 each.

Individual Canapé Plate
No. 27001

With this smart looking canapé plate you can hold a cocktail, a canapé and a cigarette in one hand and shake hands with the other. The tray has a rimmed circle in it to hold the glass from sliding around. 6¼ inches in diameter. Designed by Guild. Packed in gift box. Price, $1.00 each.

Informal Serving Tray
No. 09012

The combination of an oval exterior and an oblong interior with rounded corners gives this comparatively small 15 inch over-all tray much more carrying room than is apparent. The recessed bottom provides a deep ridge ½ inch high which prevents glasses from sliding over the edges. Finished in gleaming polished chromium or polished copper. Price, $2.50 each.

Incidental Tray
No. 09015

This simple round tray can be used for many purposes—as a card tray, a cocktail service tray, or a holder for table smoking accessories. It is 8¼ inches in diameter with a rim 5/16 of an inch high. Finished in polished chromium or polished copper. Price, 50c. each.

Chase "Quiet Pool" Design

"A pebble dropped in a still pool of water creates concentric circles." This is the theme of the design of the new sandwich plate, service plates, cold meat platter and bread tray illustrated here,—all of the distinctive Chase "Quiet Pool" design, which Lurelle Guild designed for Chase. The hair line circles are sharply etched on the flat rims. The simplicity of this design assures harmony with other table pieces. The different plates and trays can be displayed together and sold separately, and give any table a great brilliance and smartness.

Service Plate
No. 27002

These are very effective when used under smaller deep-blue glass plates. White soup saucers and cups could be placed on top. 10½ inches in diameter. Price, $3.00 each. Polished chromium or satin copper finish.

Bread Tray
No. 27005

13½ inches long, 8 inches wide. Price, $3.50 each. Polished chromium finish.

Sandwich Plate
No. 27003

13 inches in diameter. Price, $4.00 each. Polished chromium or satin copper finish.

Cold Meat Platter
No. 27004

15 inches long, 9½ inches wide. Price, $4.00 each. Polished chromium finish.

SERVICE PLATE

BREAD TRAY

SANDWICH PLATE

COLD MEAT PLATTER

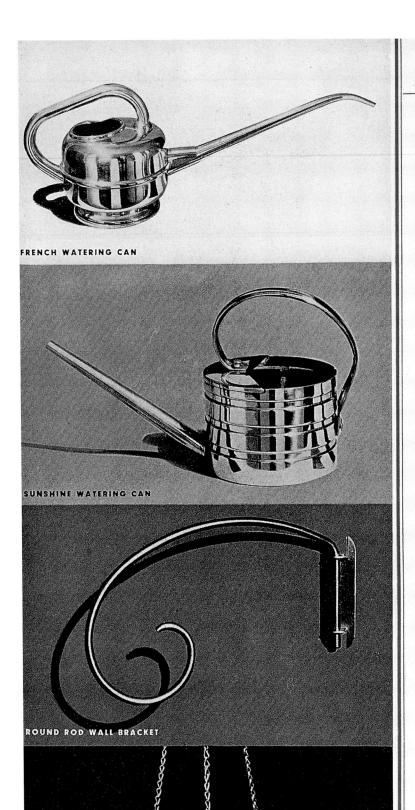

FRENCH WATERING CAN

SUNSHINE WATERING CAN

ROUND ROD WALL BRACKET

PENDANT PLANT BOWL

French Watering Can

No. 05001

An attractive European type watering can that reminds you of a cool French garden. It has a beautiful long spout curving at the end and a graceful yet sturdy handle. And it holds almost a gallon. Made in a pleasing combination of polished copper and brass, 8¼ inches high, 23 inches from handle to tip of spout. Price, $12.00 each.

Sunshine Watering Can

No. 05003

This little watering can is just the thing for watering house plants. It will reach down between the leaves to the dirt and never spill a drop. It is finished in combination polished brass and copper. Over-all length 8½ inches, height 5 inches. Price, $1.00 each.

Round Rod Wall Bracket

No. 90029

This Round Rod Wall Bracket will support pendant flower bowls, bird cages and lanterns easily and gracefully. Also an excellent support for the Chase Binnacle Light (No. 25001) illustrated on page 29. Finished in satin brass, satin copper or English bronze. The arm length is 9½ inches and hinge length 4¾ inches. Price, 75c. each.

Pendant Plant Bowl

No. 04004

An unusual design for a hanging flower bowl. The attractive ring design gives the appearance of the modern step-down effect. The chains are placed to keep the bowl hanging evenly. Depth of bowl 5½ inches, diameter 6¼ inches, height, including chain, 20 inches. Finished in polished brass; polished copper; and English bronze. Packed in a gift box Price, $1.25 each.

Tongs and Spoon Set

No. 28018

This set is particularly desirable for preparing iced drinks. It consists of a long-handled stirring spoon and a pair of ice tongs. A perfect, inexpensive bridge prize, or gift. Polished chromium finish. Per set, in attractive gift box, $1.00. Tongs only, No. 28015, 4½ inches long, 50c. Long-handled Spoon only, No. 17055, 11½ inches long, 50c.

Coaster Set

No. 11261

These coasters will not stick to their glasses. They may be had in polished copper or polished chromium. Attractively boxed in sets of four as illustrated. Price, $1.00 per set. Also sold one dozen to a box (No. 11262). Price, $3.00 per dozen.

Table Bells

No. 13006   No. 13007

These attractive table bells have a cheerful, musical ring. A useful and inexpensive gift for the dining table or the sick room. Available in polished chromium finish with either green quartz or jet black composition handles. Manchu, No. 13006, the taller of the two, is 3¼ inches high. Ming, No. 13007, with the ball knob, is 3 inches high. Price, $1.00 each.

Candy Dish

No. 90011

A candy dish with a three-compartment glass liner fitted into a well-shaped holder. The etched cover has a fruit cluster knob for a handle finished the same as the dish holder. Made in the following finishes: combination satin nickel and black; combination satin brass and copper; all satin brass; all satin copper. Diameter 7 inches, height 3¼ inches. Price, $1.00 each.

TONGS AND SPOON SET

COASTER SET

TABLE BELLS

CANDY DISH

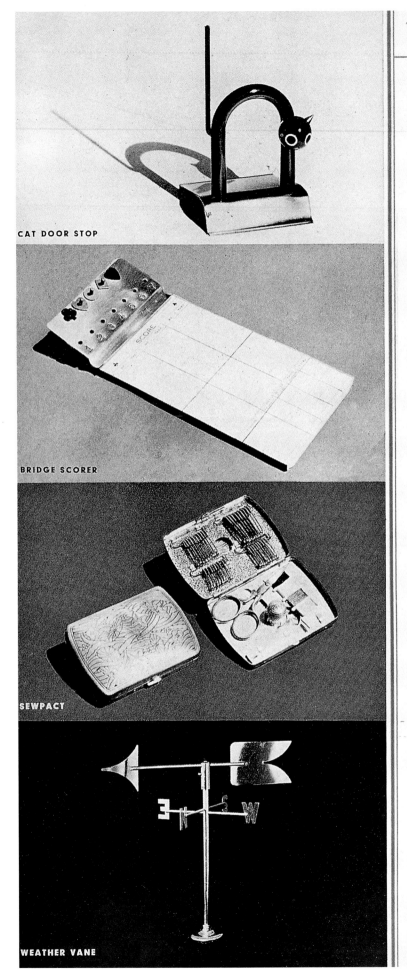

CAT DOOR STOP

BRIDGE SCORER

SEWPACT

WEATHER VANE

Cat Door Stop

No. 90035

Here's a door stop that is handsome and not fussy. A solid, handsome metal cat, dignified but humorous, will hold your door open and stop draft door slams. Combination polished brass and copper, or satin nickel and black. Height 8½ inches, width 4½ inches, depth 4¾ inches. Price, $2.00 each.

Bridge Scorer

No. 90044

This Bridge Scorer is a handy bridge accessory. The score pad is held in place by a spring clip and is easily replaced. A temporary record of the number of tricks and suit bid can be kept at the top. Size, 8 inches long, 3½ inches wide. Finished in satin brass. Price, 75c. each.

Sewpact

No. 90026

A sewing compact with an assortment of pins, a card of black, white, tan and brown thread, a pair of scissors, a thimble and a few needles. Width 2¼ inches, length 3¼ inches, thickness ¾ inch. Fits a woman's handbag, or overnight bag. Convenient to carry in car pocket. Practical for use at home and indispensable for the traveler. Made of brass and finished in satin brass, or nickel with a floral inlay of assorted colors on the cover. Packed in gift box. Price, $1.00 each.

Weather Vane

No. 90030

This all-brass non-rusting weather vane will reach the peak of many well-kept homes this year. For bathing houses, flag poles, garden houses, chicken houses, it will give its weather warnings. The graceful arrow pivots on a solid brass point enabling it to give years of service without impairing its sensitive efficiency. Height 12 inches, width 12 inches. Individually packed in box with brass screws for attaching. Price, $1.25 each.

Vanity Mirror

No. 90043

Heavily plated and buffed to perfection, this dainty metal vanity mirror has an unusually bright reflecting surface—impervious to moisture and unbreakable. The back is enameled in choice of black, white, dark brown, green, and turquoise blue etched design. Diameter 2⅜ inches. Price, 25c each.

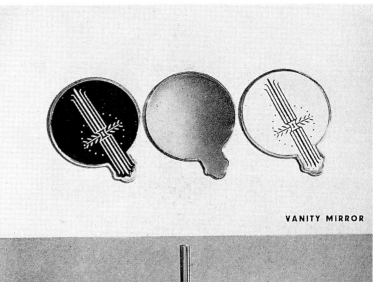

VANITY MIRROR

Four Tube Bud Holder

No. 11230

A useful, decorative holder, cleverly combining brass and copper—the center tube is of copper supplemented by brass cluster tubes. The steps of the base are alternate brass and copper. Also available in all polished chromium. For a bureau or dressing table it is just right for two or three roses, or other flowers. Height 8¼ inches, diameter 3½ inches. Individually packed. Price: combination brass and copper or chromium, $1.00 each.

FOUR TUBE BUD HOLDER

Bottle Plaques

No. 27024   No. 27025

Made with a chain to hang around the neck of decanters, these labeling plaques eliminate guesswork as to contents. Each set consists of three plaques. No. 27024, Rye, Scotch and Gin. No. 27025, Sherry, Port and Brandy. Size, 2¼ inches wide, 1⅛ inches high. Available in either polished chromium or polished copper. Black letters. Price, $1.00 per set.

BOTTLE PLAQUES

Handy Dryer

No. 11232

A practical and convenient dryer for stockings and lingerie made of brass, finished in beautiful pastel shades of blue, green, old rose and orchid. Furnished on cards as illustrated, one dozen assorted colors to a box. Price, 25c. per card.

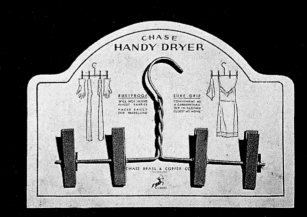

HANDY DRYER

MINT AND NUT DISH

OCCASIONAL BOX

DELTA BONBON DISH

Mint and Nut Dish

No. 29003

An unusual double dish for mints and nuts. The loop handle is lined with parallel furrows and encircles a modernistic baby whale. We have it in polished chromium finish or a combination of polished brass and copper. Overall height 4½ inches. The trays are 4 inches in diameter. Price, $2.50 each.

Occasional Box

No. 90002

A dainty little box for candy, nuts, cigarettes, or for stamps, and odds and ends on a desk top. Finished in choice of red, white, black, blue, green, or rose with colored composition knob and polished nickel trim. Comes with a white frosted glass liner. 3⅛ inches high, 4½ inches in diameter. Price, $1.00 each.

Delta Bonbon Dish

No. 28016

Here is a very attractive bonbon dish, gracefully molded, and distinctly modern because of its ribbed edge, handle and base. It is available in three finishes; satin copper and white; satin copper and green and polished chromium and black. 7 inches in diameter, 3¼ inches high. Price, $1.50 each.

Newspaper Rack

No. 27027

This amusing article is designed to hold the morning newspaper for breakfast readers. The clever cut-out rooster typifies the day's beginning. The weather vane rooster with its North, East, West and South spells out "NEWS"! This useful rack was designed for Chase by Lurelle Guild, and holds a newspaper folded in half, or quarter, at a convenient reading angle. Will also hold an ordinary sized book. 11⅜ inches high, 8⅜ inches wide, 5⅛ inches deep. English bronze or combination brass and copper finish. Price, $1.50 each.

NEWSPAPER RACK

Magazine Rack

No. 27026

Cleverly constructed of round and square wire, this magazine rack makes a most convenient receptacle for current magazines. It can be moved easily from one place to another by means of the large circular handle at the top. Another useful rack designed for Chase by Lurelle Guild. Beautifully finished in English bronze or the new smart combination of copper and white. 15⅛ inches long, 11⅛ inches high, 8⅛ inches wide. Overall height, 14 inches. Price, $9.00 each.

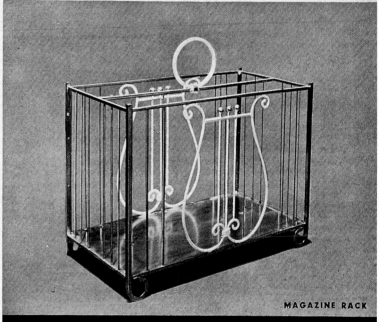

MAGAZINE RACK

Fruit Basket

No. 27028

This fruit basket designed for us by Lurelle Guild is large enough to hold a nice assortment of fruit. With a folded napkin placed inside, it is perfect to use as a cake, sandwich, or hot roll basket. The sides, made of interwined wire, flare out gently to a top rim 12½ inches in diameter. Height, including ball feet, is 4¾ inches. Finished in combination copper and white. Price, $5.00 each.

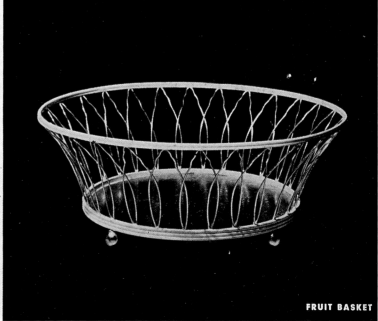

FRUIT BASKET

COLONEL LIGHT

"BOMB" FLASHLIGHT

LIGHTHOUSE LAMP

REEDED LAMP

Colonel Light

No. 27013

Here is a militant "Colonel" whose head is an electric light bulb. The tall Cossack hat is a shade that can be tilted at a cocky angle. Available in green and white, red and white, and blue and white, all combinations have black trim. Consider selling this in combination with the "Colonel's Lady Light" (on opposite page) for a child's bureau. Wired complete for plugging into regular house circuit. Height 9⅜ inches, base diameter 4 inches. Price, $2.00 each.

"Bomb" Flashlight

No. 22001

A flashlight that will stand by itself, slip over the wrist or hang from a hook. Neat and compact; fits the coat pocket, takes little space in a car pocket. Diameter 3½ inches, 1¾ inches thick. Finished in polished nickel and packed separately in an illustrated box as shown or in an attractive 3-color counter display container that holds six lights, complete with battery and bulb. Price, $1.00 each.

Lighthouse Lamp

No. 16002

A novelty lamp or electric candle in the form of a miniature lighthouse. The bulb shines brightly through the windows of the "cupola." 6⅛ inches high. Furnished in satin brass or satin nickel. Switch built in base. Complete with bulb and standard flashlight battery cells. Price, $1.00 each.

Reeded Lamp

No. 01009

A beautiful design, sparkling and smart, that blends equally well in old-fashioned and modern surroundings. The reeded pattern of the lamp standard is carried out in the parchment shade which is accordion pleated. The lamp is finished in polished copper, or white. Height 10¾ inches, base 4 inches. Price, $1.75 each.

Colonel's Lady Light

No. 27014

This demure little lady goes well in combination with the Colonel Light (see opposite page). The construction is similar to that of the Colonel Light. The bulbs are standard bulbs available everywhere. Supplied in green and white, red and white, and blue and white—all combinations with black trim. Complete with wire for plugging into house circuit. Height 9⅜ inches, base diameter 4 inches. Price, $2.00 each.

"Airalite"

No. 22003

A smart and handy companion to the powder compact; a small vest pocket flashlight. It measures but 2 x 2½ inches. It hangs on a hook or stands on its own base. Finished in polished nickel with colored inlays. Has unbreakable lens. Packed in individual gift box, or six Airalites to a display card designed for window or show case use. Complete with standard pen-light battery and bulb. Price, 75c. each.

Drum Lamp

No. 01010

Soft diffused light comes through the frosted glass "drum heads" of this novelty night lamp. The light can be directed or thrown away from the bed. The drum is 3½ inches in diameter and 3¼ inches deep. Finishes: blue bands, red body, white cord; black bands, white body, black cord; red bands, blue body, white cord. Complete with inbuilt switch and grey silk electric wire. For use on regular house current. Price, $1.50 each.

Binnacle Lights

Nos. 25001—25002

A small, brass finished lamp in a nautical design, either complete with flashlight batteries or wired for electricity, and complete with bulb. It gives sufficient illumination for a porch or hall. Equipped with frosted glass globe. It may be carried in the hand, hung on a hook, or set on the table. Height 5½ inches, diameter 3¼ inches. Price: (battery equipped), No. 25001, $1.00 each; No. 25002 (wired for electricity) $1.25 each.

CHASE

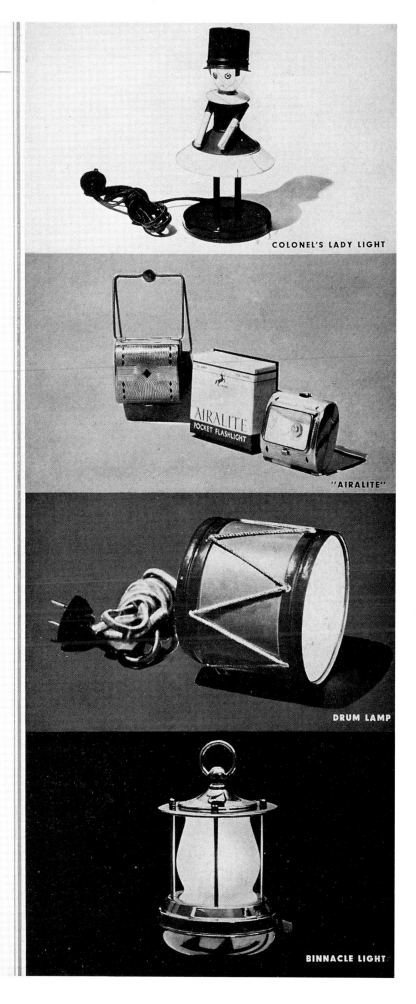

COLONEL'S LADY LIGHT

"AIRALITE"

DRUM LAMP

BINNACLE LIGHT

CONSTELLATION LAMP

DESK LAMP

BALL LAMP

CONSOLE LAMP

Constellation Lamp
No. 17048

This small lamp for the telephone table, a desk, or small occasional table is exactly right. The trim modern lines give it a sense of freshness and novelty that is very attractive. The top tilts in any direction to shade the frosted globe. Finishes; polished chromium, polished copper, antique English bronze. Height 8½ inches, diameter 7½ inches. Price, $3.00 each.

Desk Lamp
No. 01003

An attractive lamp which can be adjusted to nearly any desirable position. The shade is of very effective design in an old ivory color. Just the thing for the writing desk or reading table. Height 14½ inches, diameter 5¾ inches. Finished in English bronze or polished chromium. Price, $4.50 each.

Ball Lamp
No. 11235

A unique design in a table lamp that has definite appeal. The large circular parchment shade is decorated with parallel lines in accord with the design of the lamp body. Made in all polished chromium or a combination of polished brass and copper. Height 15 inches. Price, $7.50 each.

Console Lamp
No. 27010

While modern in design this lamp harmonizes quietly with any style of decoration. The lamp is available in choice of English bronze or satin chromium finish. The rectangular shade is striped to match the finish of the base. 17 inches high, base 5 inches wide. Price, with specially designed shade, $10.00 each.

Glow Lamp

No. 01001

This little lamp is particularly pleasing in an intimate setting. The cone-shaped top fits well down over the bulb and can be tilted at any angle. The light is reflected in a soft glow, making it ideal for a night light, or sick room use. Height with bulb 8¼ inches over-all, width 6 inches. In polished copper or combination black and chromium. Price, $1.25 each.

Circle Lamp

No. 01004

The graceful lines and exquisite finish of this modern lamp combine with the practical use for which it was designed. The shade works on a swivel which can be adjusted to any convenient angle for reading. Size: 14 inches high, 12 inches wide. Finished in polished chromium or English bronze. Complete with harmonizing shade. Price, $5.50 each.

Century Lamp

No. 01008

An up-to-date looking lamp and not too modernistic to fit in any room. The base is finished in either black or white enamel with two chromium panels. The natural parchment shade, with a sparsely stippled effect and two-half inch black bands bordered with silver, is in harmony with the base. Height 15 inches. Price, $6.00 each.

Fluted Base Table Lamp

No. 01005

Here is an unusual lamp that will harmonize with almost any period of decoration and yet be beautiful in itself. The light reflects from the polished chromium fluted sides of the base giving brilliant kaleidoscopic refractions. Height, 16 inches; diameter of shade, 12 inches. Finished in polished chromium and black. Price, $7.50 each.

GLOW LAMP

CIRCLE LAMP

CENTURY LAMP

FLUTED BASE TABLE LAMP

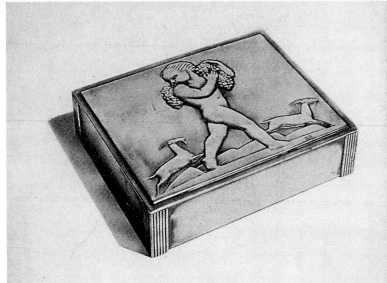

ROCKWELL KENT CIGARETTE BOX

Rockwell Kent Cigarette Box

No. 847

Rockwell Kent's famous black and white drawings are well-known in both America and Europe. We prevailed upon Mr. Kent to design for us in metal, the first time he has ever done so. This design has been beautifully reproduced by us as the cover of an exquisite bronze cigarette box. The box is lined with cedar wood and is divided into two compartments. Each of these compartments will hold fifty cigarettes of either the standard or English length. Size, 6½ inches long, 5¼ inches wide, 1⅝ inches high. Price, packed in a special gift box, $7.50 each.

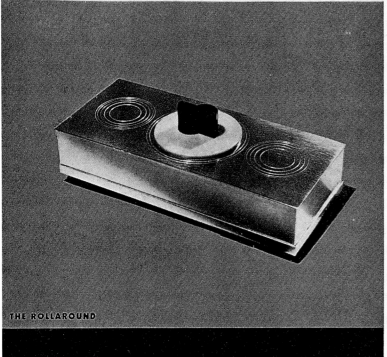

THE ROLLAROUND

The Rollaround

No. 841

A neat modern cigarette box, finished in satin nickel and mounted on four large ball bearings. It can easily be rolled across the table without marring the surface. The box is lined throughout with a wood veneer, divided into three compartments, and will hold sixty cigarettes. The top is decoratively etched with concentric circles and a splash of color is added in the composition handle. Size; 7 inches long, 3 inches wide, 1¼ inches high. Price, $2.00 each.

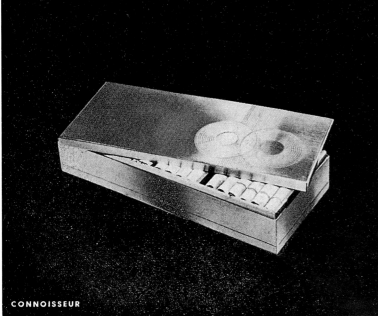

CONNOISSEUR

Connoisseur

No. 842

The cover of this cigarette box is decorated in the modern manner with hair-line geometric etchings. Inside, the box is divided into three separate wooden lined compartments which will hold twenty cigarettes each. The Connoisseur is finished in satin copper or satin nickel. It is 7 inches long, 3 inches wide and 1¼ inches high. Price, $1.25 each.

Swan Ash Tray
No. 837

So different than the usual ash tray designs that it will steal the conversation at any bridge table. The long legs with their reverse bend, the red head and solemn round black eyes are cheerful reminders to "deposit ashes here." Polished chromium finish, black head optional. Height 3 inches, width 5½ inches. Price, $1.00 each.

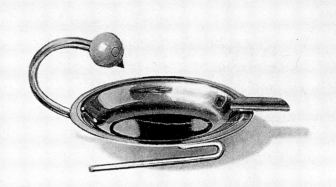

SWAN ASH TRAY

Aristocrat Ash Tray
No. 835

This ash tray makes use of some of the striking motifs of modern architecture. Strong, horizontal lines and vertical lines and reflecting flat surfaces are used. The receptacle is 1 inch deep and 4 inches in diameter. Over-all width, 5½ inches. Finishes: polished chromium, combination polished copper and brass, English bronze. Price, $1.00 each.

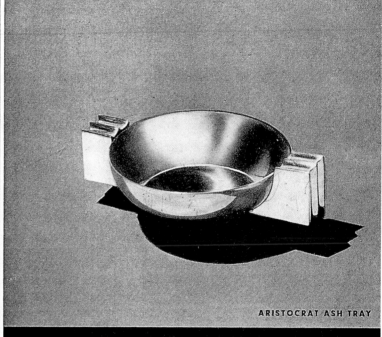

ARISTOCRAT ASH TRAY

Crown Ash Tray
No. 811

Here is a man-sized ash tray with a dumping feature which deposits ashes in a concealed, glass-lined compartment. Opens easily for cleaning. Continuous rests around upper rim. Finished in polished chromium and red, green, black, or tortoise-shell. Packed in individual gift box. Price, $2.00 each.

CROWN ASH TRAY

SUMMER ROSE ASH RECEIVER

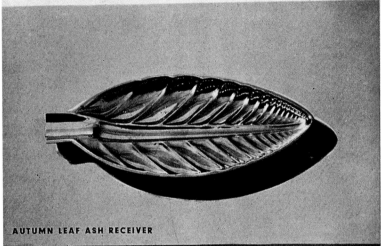

AUTUMN LEAF ASH RECEIVER

MOBY DICK ASH RECEIVER

TIP TILT ASH TRAY

Summer Rose Ash Receiver
No. 28010

A rose in full bloom reproduced in metal. The polished chromium finish makes it very easy to keep clean and looking like new. Also furnished in polished copper. 4¼ inches in diameter. Price, per set of two in gift box, $1.00.

Autumn Leaf Ash Receiver
No. 28009

Finished in choice of polished chromium, or polished copper, this ash receiver is excellent as a bridge prize, or inexpensive gift. Just right for individual use. 5 7/16 inches long. Price, per set of two in gift box, $1.00.

Moby Dick Ash Receiver
No. 28011

Surrounded by graduated ripples, this miniature whale awaits with open mouth the opportunity of holding a cigarette. Finished in combination polished chromium and black, or combination polished copper and brass. 4¼ inches in diameter. Price, 75c. each.

Tip Tilt Ash Tray
No. 819

A convenient ash tray 3¾ inches in diameter. The ashes are deposited by tilting the balanced disc on top. Available in polished nickel with either a black, green, or red stripe, around the center. Price, 30c. each. Same colors with chromium trim, 35c. each.

Shiner Ash Receiver

No. 28012

This little fish will hold plenty of cigarette ashes and his tail is formed to hold a burning cigarette. 6 5/16 inches long. Choice of polished chromium, or polished copper finishes. Price, per set of two in gift box, $1.00.

Pelican Ash Receiver

No. 17050

After depositing cigar or cigarette ashes in this amusing bird's bill, tip the bill up and the ashes will slide down inside the bird. The body separates for easy emptying. Finished in combination black and white, or black and yellow, or rose and grey. 5⅛ inches high, 7 inches long, 3⅞ inches base diameter. Price, $1.00 each.

Sextette Ash Receiver

No. 848

Six cigarette rests are formed in the top of this ash receiver. Ashes or stubs placed on the balanced disc in the center are deposited in the base by tipping the disc. Comes apart for emptying. Finishes; polished nickel, or polished copper. 3-9/16 inches diameter, 2 1/16 inches high. Price, 25c. each.

Spill-Proof Ash Receiver

No. 28013

Ashes in the roomy base of this ash receiver cannot spill out, or be blown out. The top is fitted with a balanced disc which when tilted deposits ashes in the base. The shape of the bowl prevents it from being accidentally tipped over. The bottom can be removed for emptying. Polished nickel top with black, red, or green bottom. 4 inches in diameter. Price, 25c. each.

SHINER ASH RECEIVER

PELICAN ASH RECEIVER

SEXTETTE ASH RECEIVER

SPILL-PROOF ASH RECEIVER

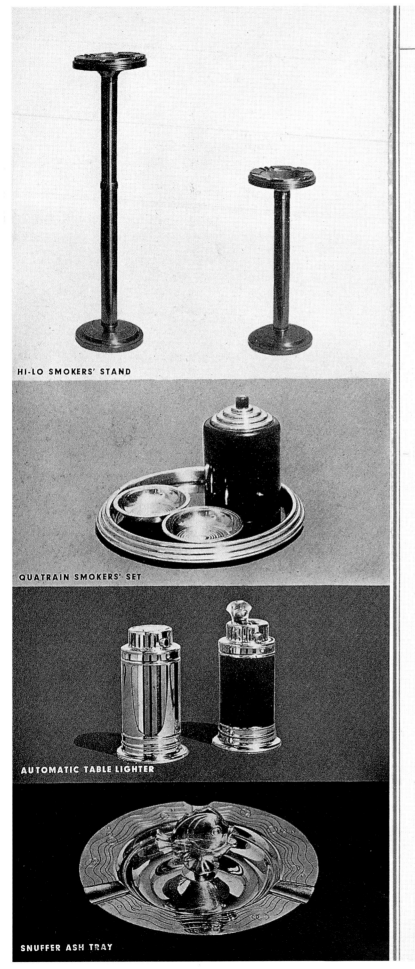

HI-LO SMOKERS' STAND

QUATRAIN SMOKERS' SET

AUTOMATIC TABLE LIGHTER

SNUFFER ASH TRAY

Hi-Lo Smokers' Stand
No. 836

The upper half of this smokers' stand telescopes into the lower half. A few turns of the ring centered on the tube holds the tray at the desired height. To empty out ashes, separate the telescopic tubes and remove cap on bottom of upper tube. Finished in English bronze or combination polished chromium and red or black enamel. Height adjustable from 16½ inches to 25½ inches. Price, $2.00 each.

Quatrain Smokers' Set
No. 28007

This modern four-piece smokers' set consists of a cigarette server and two ash trays on a glass-bottomed tray. Choice of finishes: polished nickel and red, green or black. The tray is 7 inches in diameter and the server is 3⅞ inches high. Price per set, $1.00. Set in any of these colors with polished chromium instead of nickel, $1.20 each.

Automatic Table Lighter
No. 825

This decorative table lighter lights by just pressing the button on the side of the lighter. When not in use, the mechanism is concealed under the highly polished chromium cover. The finishes are: all chromium, or chromium with black, red, green, white, or tortoise-shell enamel. 3¼ inches high, 1½ inches wide. Price, $1.00 each.

Snuffer Ash Tray
No. 845

It's fun to use this ash tray. Place the lighted end of the cigarette underneath the fish and press the fish down. The etching on the tray symbolizes ocean waves and air bubbles. 6½ inches in diameter, 2¼ inches high. Finished in all polished chromium, or chromium tray with red or black fish. Price, $1.00 each.

CHASE

Pelican Smokers' Stand

No. 17056

A very unusual bird, this pelican—he swallows cigars and cigarettes! Comfortably perched on the edge of a handy tray he rests at a very convenient height, 21 inches. The tray is 8¼ inches in diameter. Weighted base prevents tipping. Finishes: combination of black and white, black and yellow, brass and copper, English bronze. Price, $3.50 each.

Delphic Ash Receiver

No. 28008

Here is a deep bowl ash receiver with three cigarette rests that will hold an evening's consumption of cigarettes. Finished in polished chromium and black, or polished copper and black. 5⅛ inches in diameter, 1⅞ inches over-all height. Price, $1.00 each.

Cigarette Server and Ash Tray

No. 824

A combination ash tray and cigarette server that is especially shaped to fit end tables or narrow smokers' cabinets. The ash tray is of black glass 8 inches long and 4 inches wide, with three rests. The cigarette server is finished in polished nickel with either black, red, or green trim. Price, 75c. each.

Compact Cigarette Server

No. 822

A cigarette server topped with a set of four ash trays. The trays are attractively engraved on the bottom, and of convenient size for use on card tables. Available in black, white, tortoise-shell, or green, with cover and ash trays of polished chromium. Price, $1.00 each.

PELICAN SMOKERS' STAND

DELPHIC ASH RECEIVER

CIGARETTE SERVER AND ASH TRAY

COMPACT CIGARETTE SERVER

SLIDE-TOP ASH TRAYS

INDIVIDUAL ASH TRAYS

BRIDGED ASH RECEIVERS

FOUR PIECE SMOKERS' SET

Slide-Top Ash Trays
No. 804 A

Neatly packed, four to a gift box, these ash trays are fine as a bridge prize or an inexpensive gift. The bowls are of glass with sliding rims of brass on which to rest cigarettes. Polished brass tops with green glass, or polished nickel tops with black glass. Size of each tray, 3 5/16 inches long, 2⅞ inches wide, 1⅞ inches high. Price per set of four trays, 50c.

Individual Ash Trays
No. 839

These trays are available in either polished chromium or satin copper finish. They are just right for individual use at the card table. The bottoms are attractively engraved. 2¾ inches in diameter. Price, per set of four, 50c.

Bridged Ash Receivers
No. 849

This neat little set has an arresting appearance. It is finished in highly polished chromium with trays lined with black glass. The four trays nest closely together and when not in use, occupy only a small space. Trays are 3⅜ inches in diameter. Over-all height, 3¼ inches. Price, $1.00 each

Four Piece Smokers' Set
No. 823

An attractive tray 11 inches long and 5 inches wide with a modern engine-turned design on the bottom. A cigarette server and two ash trays complete this unusual value. The dome shape of the trays prevents ashes from being accidently blown or brushed off, and they can be easily taken apart for cleaning. Finished in English bronze; or polished nickel with black, red or green enamel trim. Price, $1.00 each.

Smokestack

No. 831

Modern in design, and useful on the bridge or dinner table. This cigarette container holds twenty cigarettes in a neat stack. Consider placing one at each place for the informal supper table. Bright chromium, English bronze, or black nickel finish. 3¾ inches long, 2¼ inches wide, 2 inches high. Price, $1.00 each.

SMOKESTACK

Pentad Ash Receivers

No. 840

Brilliantly finished in gleaming chromium, a set of these individual ash trays is very attractive and useful for the bridge foursome. Although they are big enough to hold plenty of ashes, they are not clumsy or top heavy. Neatly packed nests of four trays. Price, $1.00 each.

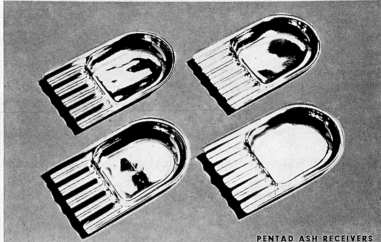

PENTAD ASH RECEIVERS

Automatic Lighter and Tray

No. 846

This is a very good-looking and useful article for the home or office. A special shelf in the center of the tray invites the replacement of the lighter after using. Furnished in all chromium finish or chromium tray with red or black automatic lighter with chromium trim. Tray is 6½ inches in diameter. 4 inches over-all height. Price, $2.00 each.

AUTOMATIC LIGHTER and TRAY

Complete Smokers' Set

No. 830

The tray of this attractive set is finished in polished chromium. A choice of green, white, tortoise-shell or black, all with chromium trim, is offered on the automatic lighter and compact cigarette server. The closely nested trays are polished chromium. Over-all dimensions: 11⅜ inches long, 5 inches wide, 3⅝ inches high. Price, $3.25 each.

COMPLETE SMOKERS' SET

CHASE

ASSEMBLY SMOKERS' SET

FLUTED ASH TRAYS

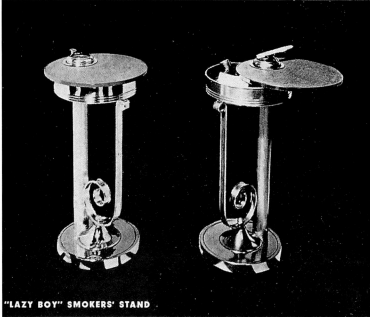

"LAZY BOY" SMOKERS' STAND

Assembly Smokers' Set

No. 850

Here is an unusual value. The set consists of an automatic lighter, a cigarette server, a set of four nested ash receivers and a large round tray. All pieces are finished in chromium except the tray which is available in green, black or red with chromium rim. Price, set complete, $2.50 each.

Fluted Ash Trays

No. 17040

A new and extremely practical ash tray. The decorative fluted edge is designed to hold a cigarette regardless of the direction from which the tray is approached. 4 inches in diameter. Finished in lustrous satin chromium, black nickel or English bronze. Neatly packed, nest of four trays. Price, $1.00 each.

"Lazy Boy" Smokers' Stand

No. 17031

This beautiful combination of ash stand and smokers' cabinet is dignified and serious enough for a man's office and yet handsome enough for the most luxurious living room. The chromium and red combination is very decorative in game rooms, porches and modern rooms. It has a roomy compartment for pipes, tobacco, cigars, cigarettes, and matches, which is easily accessible by sliding open the top which pivots around the ash tray. The special composition top is stainproof to insure a permanently neat and trim appearance. The base is heavily weighted to prevent tipping. The ash container runs the length of the corrugated tube and can easily be emptied by lifting up the ash tray and tube. A spring attached to the cover of the ash receiver keeps it tightly closed when not in use. This clever and useful smokers' stand was designed for us by Walter Von Nessen. Finishes: English bronze with top to match, combination black and satin nickel with black top and chromium with red top. Over-all height, 22 inches; top diameter, 14 inches. Price, $12.50 each.

CHROMIUM

AND

COPPER

FINISHES

Chase products come to you properly finished for their use.

We are adding a few words of explanation here of these finishes and their care.

Copper Finish

Many Chase products are finished in polished or satin copper. In all cases the word "Copper" is used to designate the finish of the article, and not necessarily the basic metal underneath. While the basic metal used is always a non-rustable copper, or copper alloy, we have in many cases slightly alloyed the copper at an extra expense in order to give additional strength and hardness. Pure copper, although cheaper, is apt to be a little soft for such uses as beer mugs and bowls, and the addition of another metal greatly increases the tensile strength and hardness of the finished product, making it less liable to dent or bend even with hard usage.

Chase Chromium

Chromium is not a basic metal as many people suppose, but an extremely hard and durable finish that is plated over a brass or copper base that has first been nickel plated.

It should require no polishing, and no abrasive powders or cleaning liquids should be used. If the product is washed in soap and water and rubbed briskly with a dry cloth, the chromium finish should retain a permanent lustre and brilliance.

CHASE

Index & Price Guide

About the Index

Thirty-three items appeared only in the 1934 Chase catalog, with an additional sixty-seven making their debut in 1935. Eighty-six items appeared in both catalogs. As the original catalog page numbers are used in this reprint, the Index has been arranged by item number, beginning with the lowest. (The Chase penchant for assigning an inventory number for each variation of an object is particularly helpful to collectors.) Any inventory number or name variations occurring after 1935 are not included in this publication.

For easy reference, the page numbers on which an object can be found in each year's catalog are given alongside the item description.

About the Price Guide

Price research for this Guide was coordinated by Barry L. Van Hook of the Chase Collectors Society. The estimates are a composite of actual current selling prices, and may vary according to locale and demand.

Price ranges given are for Chase items in "excellent" condition. Mr. Van Hook defines the term as follows:

- First and foremost, the piece contains *all* original elements as manufactured
- All original plating is intact with NO underlying metal showing through the plating
- The piece shows minimal surface marking or imperfections from handling and use, and no mark, imperfection, or scratch can be felt with a fingernail
- Any plastic, glass, or wood fitments are free from chips, cracks or scratches
- Any painted surface is intact and free of chips or flaking
- With the exception of lamps initially sold with fabric, parchment or paper shades, original shades are present

The following considerations may also impact value either positively or negatively, and should be noted:

- Items displaying flaws which cause them to be graded less than excellent, (as defined above), should be valued *significantly less*.
- Unless otherwise indicated, there is little or no difference

in value among chrome, copper, or brass versions of an item. However, those finished in "English Bronze" may be less desirable than the polished versions.
- Most of the plastic elements on Chase products were originally white. Over the years, environmental factors altered the original color to shades ranging from pale yellow to dark amber. Lighter shades tend to be preferable, with white or almond most desired.
- Items found in unused condition, in their original boxes, may bring a premium of perhaps 50 to 100 percent above suggested prices.

Several items have not been priced, but are instead captioned "No Data." These objects made only brief appearances in the Chase line, and today surface very infrequently, even among seasoned Chase collectors. Due to these factors, as well as a lack of similar products in the inventory, it is impossible to price them with any degree of accuracy. Certainly the items are "rare" in the sense that they are seldom encountered. This is not, however, the same as intrinsic worth; some, such as lampshades and pinpacks, were simply not durable enough to last the years. In any event, no attempt has been made to "set" what would only, at present, be an artificial value on these pieces. (Naturally, a collector stumbling across a "no data" item would very likely be pleased to acquire it. The monetary value of such a lucky find would then depend primarily on the collector's desire for a comprehensive Chase collection.)

A price guide such as this can assist the collector in differentiating the commonplace from the rare, and is most effective when viewed as a reference point to begin negotiations. Lower or higher prices will be dictated by the individual sales situation, and neither the authors nor the publisher can guarantee specific outcomes. We do, however, guarantee you'll enjoy the quest for Chase. Our best wishes for success!

For information on the Chase Collectors Society, please contact:

Barry L. Van Hook,
2149 W. Jibsail Loop
Mesa, AZ 85202-5524
phone: (602) 838-6971
e-mail: vanhook@asu.edu

ITEM #:	ITEM:	1934 Catalog	1935 Catalog	Price Range:
NS-287	TRAY (ROUND, 12") (same as 17006)	11		$70-80
500	HUMPTY DUMP ASH TRAY	41		$50-60
804 A	SLIDE TOP ASH TRAYS (SET OF 4)		38	$70-80
806	CIGARETTE SERVER AND ASH TRAY (ROUND)	46		$40-45
809	ECLIPSE ASH TRAY	42		$65-70
810	NOB-TOP ASH TRAY	43		$35-45
811	CROWN ASH TRAY	45	33	$45-55
815	DE LUXE CIGARETTE SET	46		$70-80
819	TIP TILT ASH TRAY	40	34	$40-50
820	MATCH-PACK ASH TRAY (SET OF 4)	45		$50-60
821	ROUNDABOUT ASH TRAY	40		$65-75
822	COMPACT CIGARETTE SERVER	44	37	$60-70
823	FOUR PIECE SMOKERS' SET	45	38	$70-80
824	CIGARETTE SERVER & ASH TRAY (8" x 4")	41	37	$100-110
825	AUTOMATIC TABLE LIGHTER	44	36	$40-50
828	AUTOMATIC LIGHTER & TRAY (#810 NOB-TOP PATTERN)	46		$65-75
830	COMPLETE SMOKERS' SET		39	$100-110
831	SMOKESTACK	41	39	$70-80
835	ARISTOCRAT ASH TRAY	40	33	$40-50
836	HI-LO SMOKERS' STAND	42	36	$120-130
837	SWAN ASH TRAY	44	33	$80-90
839	INDIVIDUAL ASH TRAYS (SET OF 4)		38	$35-45
840	PENTAD ASH RECEIVERS (SET OF 4)	43	39	$45-55
841	THE ROLLAROUND red handle:	39	32	$90-100
	blue, yellow or black:			$100-130
842	CONNOISSEUR		32	$70-80
844	THE "FOURSOME" ASH RECEIVER SET	40		$80-100
845	SNUFFER ASH TRAY		36	$60-70
846	AUTOMATIC LIGHTER & TRAY (#845 SNUFFER PATTERN)		39	$65-75
847	ROCKWELL KENT CIGARETTE BOX		32	$1000-1200
848	SEXTETTE ASH RECEIVER		35	$40-50
849	BRIDGED ASH RECEIVERS (SET OF 4)		38	$50-60
850	ASSEMBLY SMOKERS' SET		40	$120-130
1001	DUPLEX PINPACK	37		NO DATA
1001 A	DUPLEX PINPACK DISPLAY CABINET	37		NO DATA
1002 A	THE VANITY ARISTOCRAT	37		NO DATA
01001	GLOW LAMP	30	31	$70-80

ITEM #:	ITEM:	1934 Catalog	1935 Catalog	Price Range:
01003	DESK LAMP	30	30	$70-80
01004	CIRCLE LAMP	31	31	$70-80
01005	FLUTED BASE TABLE LAMP	30	31	$100-120
01006	SHIP AHOY LIGHT	31		$70-80
01007	TANKARD LAMP	32		$70-80
01008	CENTURY LAMP	32	31	$100-120
01009	REEDED LAMP	32	28	$70-80
01010	DRUM LAMP		29	$150-170
03005	TROPHY VASE	20	10	$70-80
03006	VICTORIAN VASE	21		$40-50
03007	CALYX VASE (SMALL, 6 ½" h.)	20	10	$40-50
03008	CALYX VASE (LARGE, 7 ½" h.)	20	10	$40-50
04003	RIBBED FLOWER POT	28	11	$60-70
04004	PENDANT PLANT BOWL	27	22	$40-45
05001	FRENCH WATERING CAN	26	22	$180-200
05002	RAIN-BEAU WATERING CAN	26		$50-60
05003	SUNSHINE WATERING CAN		22	$30-40
09001	TRIPLE TRAY	10	13	$20-25
09002	SERVING TRAY	12	14	$150-160
09003	FRUIT TRAY		14	$150-160
09004	TROJAN PLATE (12" d.)		20	$65-75
09009	CHEESE SERVER (COMPLETE)	8	17	$90-100
09010	CHEESE SERVER TRAY	8	17	$65-75
09011	ROUND TRAY (8 ¾" d.)	12		NO DATA
09012	INFORMAL SERVING TRAY	12	20	$65-75
09013	COCKTAIL TRAY	18	16	$35-45
09014	COASTER TRAY		16	$70-80
09015	INCIDENTAL TRAY		20	$40-45
11108	MAGNO GARDEN MARKER	27		NO DATA
11155	FLOWER POT HOLDER	28	11	$50-55
11230	FOUR TUBE BUD HOLDER	21	25	$25-35
11232	HANDY DRYER	36	25	NO DATA
11233	INDOOR FLOWER CULTIVATOR	28	11	$40-45
11235	BALL LAMP	33	30	$120-130
11261	COASTER SET (4)	10	23	$20-25
11262	COASTER SET (12)	10	23	$60-75
13002	BRITTANY TABLE BELL	17		$70-80
13003	RONDO TABLE BELL	17		$70-80

ITEM #:	ITEM:	1934 Catalog	1935 Catalog	Price Range:
13004	CUCKOO TABLE BELL	17		$70-80
13005	APOLLO TABLE BELL	17		$70-80
13006	MANCHU TABLE BELL		23	$50-60
13007	MING TABLE BELL		23	$50-60
15003	IMPERIAL BOWL	20	9	$120-130
15004	PRETZEL BOWL	24	18	$60-70
16002	LIGHTHOUSE LAMP		28	$90-100
17006	ROUND TRAY (12" d.) (same as NS-287)		13	$70-80
17007	FRUIT BOWL		11	$100-120
17026	TAVERN PITCHER	25		$230-250
17027	TIFFIN TRAY	11	13	$180-200
17029	DIPLOMAT COFFEE SET (NO TRAY)	17	12	$280-300
17030	DIPLOMAT TRAY	17	12	$230-250
17031	"LAZY BOY" SMOKERS' STAND	47	40	$400-450
17039	RING VASE	21	10	$45-55
17040	FLUTED ASH TRAYS (4)	43	40	$40-50
17045	LOTUS SAUCE BOWL	8	12	$40-45
17046	VIKING SAUCE BOWL	8	12	$45-50
17048	CONSTELLATION LAMP	31	30	$230-250
17049	STIRRING COCKTAIL MIXER		17	$90-110
17050	PELICAN ASH RECEIVER		35	$140-150
17051	CONTINENTAL COFFEE POT		6	$175-200
17052	CONTINENTAL SUGAR BOWL		6	$20-25
17053	CONTINENTAL CREAM PITCHER		6	$20-25
17054	CONTINENTAL COFFEE-MAKING SERVICE (3-PIECE)		6	$210-250
17055	LONG-HANDLED SPOON (FROM #28018 SET)		23	$40-45
17056	PELICAN SMOKERS' STAND		37	$350-400
21003	MIRROR TOP BOX	38		$900-1000
22001	"BOMB" FLASHLIGHT	34	28	$45-65
22003	"AIRALITE"	34	29	$75-80
24002	SUNDAY SUPPER CANDLE HOLDERS (4)	16	10	$35-45
24003	TAUREX CANDLESTICK (EVEN)	16	9	$75-80
24004	TAUREX CANDLESTICK (UNEVEN)	16	9	$75-80
24005	DISC CANDLESTICK	16	9	$250-270
24006	CHASE MECHANICAL CANDLE, 10 ½" h.		7	NO DATA
24007	CHASE MECHANICAL CANDLE, 7" h.		7	NO DATA
25001	BINNACLE LIGHT (BATTERY)	35	29	$35-40
25002	BINNACLE LIGHT (WIRED)	35	29	$35-40

ITEM #:	ITEM:	1934 Catalog	1935 Catalog	Price Range:
26001	BREAKFAST SET (WITHOUT TRAY)	9	14	$35-40
26002	COCKTAIL CUP	18	18	$5-6
26003	BREAKFAST SET (COMPLETE)	9	14	$40-50
27001	INDIVIDUAL CANAPE PLATE	11	20	$15-20
27002	SERVICE PLATE	13	21	$40-50
27003	SANDWICH PLATE	13	21	$50-60
27004	COLD MEAT PLATTER	13	21	$60-70
27005	BREAD TRAY	13	21	$50-60
27006	SALAD BOWL	9		NO DATA
27007	"ARCHITEX" CANDLESTICK	15	8	$50-60
27008	"ARCHITEX" CENTERPIECE (CIRCULAR)	15	8	$50-60
27009	"ARCHITEX" CENTERPIECE (RECTANGULAR)	15	8	$50-60
27010	CONSOLE LAMP	33	30	$300-325
27011	ELECTRIC BUFFET SERVER (110 VOLTS)	6	4	$150-175
27012	"ARCHITEX" ADJUSTABLE CENTERPIECE (COMPLETE)	14	8	$550-600
27013	COLONEL LIGHT	35	28	$275-300
27014	COLONEL'S LADY LIGHT		29	$275-300
27015	WINE COOLER		15	$550-600
27016	WINE BOTTLE STAND		15	$450-500
27024	BOTTLE PLAQUES (3) (RYE, SCOTCH, GIN)		25	$80-90
27025	BOTTLE PLAQUES (3) (SHERRY, PORT, BRANDY)		25	$80-90
27026	MAGAZINE RACK		27	NO DATA
27027	NEWSPAPER RACK		27	$40-45
27028	FRUIT BASKET		27	NO DATA
27030	ATHENA CANDELABRA		7	$250-275
28001	COCKTAIL CANAPE SERVER		15	$175-200
28002	ICE BOWL AND TONGS		17	$65-75
28003	PANCAKE AND CORN SET		14	$200-250
28004	SALT AND PEPPER SPHERES		14	$50-60
28005	PANCAKE AND CORN PITCHER		14	$90-100
28007	QUATRAIN SMOKERS' SET		36	$200-225
28008	DELPHIC ASH RECEIVER		37	$60-70
28009	AUTUMN LEAF ASH RECEIVER		34	$40-45
28010	SUMMER ROSE ASH RECEIVER		34	$40-45
28011	MOBY DICK ASH RECEIVER		34	$45-50
28012	SHINER ASH RECEIVER		35	$50-60
28013	SPILL-PROOF ASH RECEIVER		35	$50-60
28014	"HIGH-HAT" JIGGER		18	$15-20

ITEM #:	ITEM:	1934 Catalog	1935 Catalog	Price Range:
28015	TONGS (FROM #28018 SET)		23	$40-45
28016	DELTA BONBON DISH		26	$70-80
28017	JIGGER AND SWIZZLER SET		18	$60-70
28018	TONGS AND SPOON SET		23	$80-90
29001	FIESTA CANDLESTICKS		8	$165-175
29002	FIESTA FLOWER BOWL		8	$80-90
29003	MINT AND NUT DISH		26	$30-40
90002	OCCASIONAL BOX	38	26	$50-60
90003	HANDY DRYER (4)	36		NO DATA
90004	SALEM WATER PITCHER	25		$130-150
90006	HOT SERVICE COVER, (SMALL, 7 ¼" d.)	10		$40-50
90007	HOT SERVICE COVER, (LARGE, 8 ½" d.)	10		$50-60
90010	SALVER		13	$200-225
90011	CANDY DISH	19	23	$20-25
90018	JAM SET clear/chrome: pink/copper:	9	12	 $40-45 $80-100
90025	DEVONSHIRE PITCHER	25	19	$75-85
90026	SEWPACT	36	24	NO DATA
90027	CONFECTION BOWL	19		$70-80
90029	ROUND ROD WALL BRACKET	27	22	NO DATA
90030	WEATHER VANE	29	24	$225-250
90031	CHESHIRE MUG	23	19	$30-40
90032	BACCHUS GOBLET	23	19	$25-35
90033	FOOT SCRAPER	29		NO DATA
90034	COCKTAIL SHAKER (later named "GAIETY")	18	16	$40-45
90035	CAT DOOR STOP	29	24	$200-230
90036	BACCHUS PITCHER	24	19	$150-160
90037	NIBLICK SWIZZLERS (4)	19	18	$40-45
90038	PRETZELMAN copper: chrome:	24	18	 $100-120 $180-200
90042	BEER MUG	23		$25-30
90043	VANITY MIRROR	36	25	NO DATA
90044	BRIDGE SCORER		24	NO DATA
90046	LIQUEUR SET		16	$165-180
90047	LIQUEUR CUPS (6)		16	$90-100
90048	ELECTRIC SNACK SERVER		5	$90-100
90049	"VICTORY" SHADE		7	NO DATA
90050	"TALISMAN" SHADE		7	NO DATA